SPEAKING EASY

How to speak to your audiences
with confidence and authority
(Edition three)

Michael Brown

Media Associates
Christchurch, New Zealand

Speaking Easy
How to speak to your audiences with confidence and authority
Edition three
© Michael Brown 2008
Illustrations Tim Tripp
ISBN 978-0-473-13154-8

Edition one: Media Associates (Christchurch) 1996
Edition two: Media Associates (Christchurch) 2001
Edition three: Media Associates (Christchurch) 2008

Publisher's details:
Media Associates of New Zealand Limited,
PO Box 1142, Christchurch, New Zealand.
Ph 64-3-3653164. Fax 64-3-3662896.
info@media-associates.co.nz
www.media-associates.co.nz

All rights reserved. This work is subject to copyright and no part may be reproduced or transmitted in any form or by any means, electronic or mechanical, including photocopying, recording, storage in any information retrieval system or otherwise without the written permission of the author.

Companion books from the same publisher:

Media Easy
How to handle the news media with confidence and authority

Making Business Writing Easy
What effective business writers really do

Success at Work and at Home
A *how to* book to help you become a more successful businessperson, partner, coach, parent, colleague, scholar, sportsperson and friend

CONTENTS

1 How do I turn this book into real skills? 1

Getting personal authority by giving fundamental respect 4
Leadership 5
Which part of your speech carries the greatest impact? 5
Making fear work for you 9
Two life choices 12
Passionate visualization: how to programme your subconscious 14

2 How do I prepare? 19

Ask the how/what/where questions 19
Ask the crunch audience questions 20
The four-step, all-purpose preparation (the city model) 22
Rehearse the order of delivery 34
Don't write prompt notes to be hand-held 35
If you must read out a fully written speech 36
Summary 39
How to prepare for a difficult audience 40
In the hours before 40
The final count-down 44
How to overcome persistent symptoms of fear 46
For the truly terrified 47

3 How do I make my audio-visual aids effective? 53

How to prepare 54
How to deliver visual aids to an audience 57

4 How do I work out my personal performance key? 65

5 How do I become more persuasive and convincing? 79

Build rapport right at the beginning 79
Signpost your presentation 80
Give them variety 80
Improve your persuasiveness by blirting 81
How to handle embarrassing mistakes 81
Be open, but not an open book 83
When your personal views conflict with your message 84
Keep your body language open 85
Look at everyone with your chest 86
Sitting presenters—sit up 87
The power of silence 87
Bigger audiences want *you* to be bigger 88
Your notes and the lectern 89
Tell stories to make your message memorable 90
Make humour work for you 92
Signals to journalists 95
How to apologize or admit a mistake 96
Never, ever, apologize for your speaking abilities 97
Speak the language of real people 98

6 How do I handle questions and interjections? 101

Listen on behalf of everyone 102
Share the reply, showing warmth, interest and energy 103
Accept feelings, argue facts 108
How to handle a persistent interjector 113
How to handle audience anger when you deserve it 114
Answering closed questions 115
When the interjection doesn't need verbal attention 116

Handling the hidden agenda 116
Handling cross-fire 118
When there's an expert in the audience 119
When you don't know the answer 121
When the farewelled one bites back 121
Dealing with a drunk interjector 122
Handling a heckler 123

7 How do I handle formal or special occasions? 125

Formal salutations 125
Introducing a speaker 126
Thanking a speaker 127
Farewelling a staff member or colleague 128
Presenting and receiving awards 130
Opening functions 131
Funerals 131
Other family and friends speeches 133

Selected quotable quotes 137

BIBLIOGRAPHY 159

 # How do I turn this book into real skills?

Fear, flying, and the art of convincing an audience

Recently I caught a cab from Wellington Airport into the city. The Fijian-Indian driver rode in silence, until we were in the middle of Victoria Tunnel. Then he looked at me in his mirror.
"What do you do, sir?" he asked.
"I teach presentation skills."
The effect on him was electric. Actually it was my hair that stood on end, because in the middle of the tunnel, in peak-hour, bumper-to-bumper traffic, he lifted both hands off the wheel and waved them about in the air.
"Speaking in public!" he shouted, "I love speaking in public!"
When his hands returned to the wheel and my face regained it's normal hue, I learned that when he was nine years old—back in Fiji—he had seen a powerful speaker and thought, *One day, I will be him.* Now, he constantly looked for opportunities to speak to family, friends, sporting colleagues and at church. Any occasion would do.
In the West, that attitude is rare. Speaking in public is counted as one of the most terrifying of all social activities.
Yet it can so easily be fun, deeply satisfying, even thrilling, and a fast track to personal authority throughout our lives. I want to show you how to get all of that and more, even as you reduce the fear to no more than useful, nervous adrenaline. We'll look at your beliefs about yourself, how to prepare, how to perform, and how to interact with your audiences.
You have chosen an excellent era to tackle this wonderful skill, because Western work and business cultures have begun to value the very qualities you'll need. Over the last few decades, the way we interact and work together has been going through a radical change. It's a paradigm shift so significant that future generations will look back and recognize the birth struggles of the civilization we thought we had already. Mahatma Gandhi might well agree, because when he was asked what he thought of Western civilization, he replied, "I believe it would be a very good idea." That good idea is forming.
Here's one indicator. The Huthwaite Group conducted comprehensive international research—involving no less than 10,000 salespeople in 50

companies and 23 countries—and found that the most successful sales method had an interesting component: genuine interest in the customer. Yes, you read that correctly. The fact that such a result is a 'discovery' indicates something of the change under way. The same study found that for larger sales, many of the hallowed methods of manipulating people never worked in the long term and were only kept pumping by anecdotal evidence. Believe it or not, twentieth century people-management systems and models grew from military models because—it was presumed—the military were the only organizations that knew how to get people to do the necessary.

You see what this means? Whatever your techniques and strategies, whatever your short term gains, most people, most of the time, somehow know how genuine you are. They know if you have their interests at heart.

Forbes magazine says the sharks are learning how to succeed in business by being nice to their competitors. Herb Cohen's world best-seller *You Can Negotiate Anything* is dedicated to a man whose negotiating strategy was to always give much more than he received. Steven Covey's *Seven Habits of Highly Effective People* says that in the long run we cannot succeed with strategies to influence people if our character is fundamentally flawed.

Character? It suggests that at some level, people know what we are.

At levels ranging from gut feeling to subconscious—they do. And when we speak in front of an audience the effect is even greater, because the group consciousness is more than a collection of individual minds and is more able to sense our inner strengths and weaknesses. Deep down we know that. The implications for leadership and the management of people are staggering. And so are the implications for the way we set out to persuade, convince and inform people who gather in one place to listen to us.

So what are you?

If you would understand what you are, you might start with what you believe about yourself and about others.

What we believe most deeply about ourselves and others has a profound subconscious impact on our audiences.

Are you still there? Excellent, because the good news outweighs the bad. I know, this is getting in deeper than you might have expected, but stay with me because this thinking is going to give real power to the practical tips and suggestions ahead.

- want to be here talking to us.
- want to be where they are right now.

Of course effective presenters don't talk about any of that. They don't need to. They've simply chosen to adopt those attitudes and when we're in their audience we sense such attitudes and are attracted by them, even though we may never know consciously what it is that attracts us.

We can all think of hugely influential speakers—John Kennedy, Winston Churchill, Martin Luther King—but it's too easy to make their abilities unreachable with words like charisma, or the 'X' factor, as if they were some mysterious quality you need to be born with. You don't. Churchill certainly wasn't born with it: he suffered badly from speaker's nerves (see p11).

I know from my workshops that most people don't want to become brilliant, ball-of-fire orators; they just want to be good enough to look confident, credible and authoritative. You can easily achieve that and—if you want—much, much more. Strong personal authority is inherent in all of us, waiting to be developed.

How do we get it? The rest of this book answers that question, and it starts with something you give.

Getting personal authority by giving fundamental respect

Fundamental respect is the undercurrent of respect you feel for every individual, regardless of circumstance. Perhaps it is because they occupy the same planet, or perhaps because they breathe the same air as you do. Put it your own way. It's subtle, it's never spoken, it's what Nicola did. It's how to begin building your personal authority.

That may seem strange when Mick Jones back there in the fourth row keeps interjecting aggressively, picks his nose, and is known to borrow money from the charity box in the café. But I'm not suggesting you have to like what he does. Fundamental respect has little to do with what others do and say, it has little to do with 'like' and 'dislike', 'agree' and 'disagree', 'with us' and 'against us'.

Fundamental respect does not come and go with the breeze.

It does not judge what other people are.

It does not judge what you are.

It values people because they are people.

Your audiences will sense it in you. And this should sound familiar now; at some level, they know and they cannot help but be influenced.

In an old Wayne and Schuster skit, Dr Tex Rorschach (*Frontier Psychiatrist*) interviews a patient lying on a saloon bar.

Patient: You mean if I like them, they're going to like me?

Dr R: Siggie Freud couldn't have put it better.

My most significant interview in 15 years of broadcasting taught me the same point. I was talking to a dying five-year-old girl. Nicola had terminal muscular atrophy. She was still well enough to be at school, though in a wheelchair. She was extraordinarily popular with her classmates, winning their respect and attention far beyond any sense of pity or duty. In the middle of the interview I commented on her popularity. Recognizing my words as a question, she screwed up her face to think about it.

Then she said, "I think it's because I like them." That from a five-year-old.

Liking—of others and of ourselves—is a vital component of personal authority.

Personal authority has nothing to do with power or positional authority—nothing to do with your title, or rank, or the letters after your name. It has nothing to do with the company you keep, your income, the clothes you wear, the car you drive, or the house you live in. Nor is it something you have to be born with.

Personal authority is a coin with two equally important sides. The first is *connected* personal authority: the ability to connect with other people. It's what Nicola had. But don't think for one moment that I'm suggesting sainthood as a pre-requisite, because the second type of personal authority has nothing to do with good, bad, or ethics: it's *separate* personal authority—the individual strength to stand alone.

Presenters with connected personal authority give us the feeling that they:	Presenters with separate personal authority give us the feeling that they:
• know our strengths and weaknesses and are comfortable with them.	• know their own strengths and weaknesses and are comfortable with them.
• believe in our potential.	• believe in their own potential
• respect us.	• respect themselves.
• want us to feel passionate about their topic, yet respect our right and ability to make up our own minds.	• feel passionately about their topic. They know their own minds.

Make no mistake, there's nothing wimpish about fundamental respect. As you'll see, you can assertively disagree with someone in public while practising it. You can have a boisterous argument with an entire audience and they will respect you because they can sense your fundamental respect for them. The same principle operates in all person-to-person contacts. You can fire someone while practising it and, in spite of the pain involved, that person is likely to go away respecting you.

Those who cultivate fundamental respect for others cannot help but emanate strength and presence. Even audiences who oppose your message will be drawn to you and usually they won't know why.

Leadership

This book is not about another management skill. It's about the verbal, vocal and body language of leadership. When major companies hire a top executive, what attribute do you think is number one on their priority list? Ability to organize? Ability to draft good policy? Ability to see a clear vision and plot a course to it? Certainly they're important, but number one is something else: the ability to persuade, convince and inspire the people who run the ship so that it sails smoothly on.

Speak well in front of others and you are noted, consciously or subconsciously by your audiences, as someone who is destined for higher things. For the ambitious, learning to speak in public is the fast track to respect, admiration and promotion.

Even for those who simply want to survive the experience intact, learning to speak in public is a fast track to self esteem. And the amazing thing is that it's *not* difficult; you only need to realize that it's a mind game you can master.

Which part of your speech carries the greatest impact?

Let's make two assumptions: that feelings and attitudes are important for conveying facts, and that facts are rarely perceived as emotionally neutral.

With those same assumptions, psychologist Albert Mehrabian analysed the way a speaker's attitudes and feelings impact on a listener. He asked what proportion of the perceived attitudes/feelings are in the *verbal* content (the meaning of the words)? How much is in the *visual* content (body language)? And how much is in the *vocal* content (tones)? In other words he wanted to know which part of speech carries the greatest impact.

6   How do I turn this book into real skills?

He predicted that 50% of the impact would be in content, 30% visual and 20% vocal. But the results were startlingly different.[1]

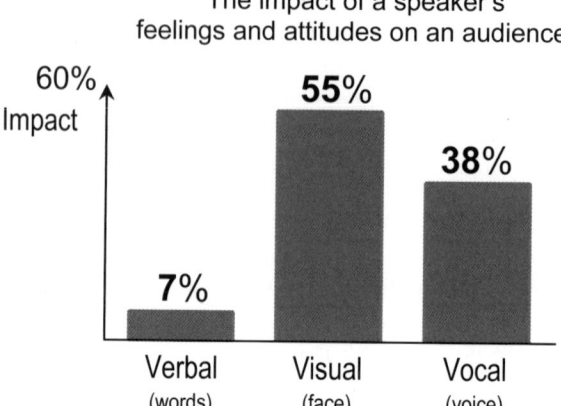

If we combine the last two columns, we get this:

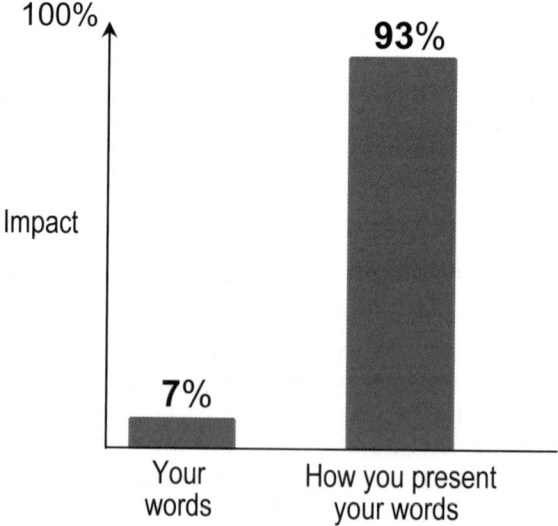

---

[1] Mehrabian & Ferris, Journal of Consulting Psychology, Vol. 31, 1967.

That experiment assumed an audience of one, but everything in my acting, broadcasting and speaking experience says that the general principle still applies. The conclusion is inescapable:

Your ability to persuade and convince
depends much more on how you deliver the message,
than on the message.

Some find that annoying. Surely the content is the most important. Well, of course it is. But we're not talking about the importance of your message, we're talking about the impact of your message.

It's not what you tell them that counts, it's what they take away.

The same point is made by the story of a small boy who boasted to his brothers—and bet a shilling on it—that he had taught the dog how to sing. When they demanded proof, the dog could only bark. But the boy was unruffled and insisted that he had won the bet. 'I only said I had taught him,' he said. 'I didn't say he learned anything.'

Late last century, a man called Elliot was diagnosed with a tumour between the left and right hemispheres of his brain. Keep in mind that the left brain is our main source of decision-making, and the right brain our main source of feelings. He had the tumour removed by a surgeon called Antonio Damasio.[2] It seemed a completely successful operation.

But it wasn't, because Elliot's life soon fell apart. He lost his career—he was a lawyer—his investments, and his marriage, and he moved into a room in his brother's house. Also, his friends and relatives noticed two strange behaviours. First, he could not seem to make decisions, even for something as simple as his next appointment (left brain). Second, he didn't seem to have any feelings (right brain); Damasio was more upset by what had happened to Elliot than Elliot was. What was going on?

So the research began. In Elliot's case, the surgery had not damaged the left or the right brain, but it had severed some of the links between the two. Think of it as links between decision-making and feelings, and you'll see where this is going. The findings come in two parts and they may be the most profound discovery ever made about what drives human decisions:

- We cannot make a decision without involving our feelings.

---

[2] Source *Descartes' Error*, Antonio Damasio 1996

- Feelings come first, then the decisions (one thousandth of a second later).

In other words, reason needs—and follows—passion. Reason cannot operate in isolation. Now we know why that huge difference between the impact of what you say and the impact of how you say it.

> The decision your audience makes about your message depends much more on their feelings than their logic.

Can you imagine anything more significant for a presenter? This is surely the end of thinking that delivering the facts will do the job. It can be sobering for people in fact-based disciplines to realize that it's feelings, not logic, that engage their audiences.

One reservation: if your audience has a specific interest in the message, it will—up to a point—make an effort to penetrate poor presentation to get the content. For such audiences, that figure of seven per cent is surely too low.

Even so, consider this. In my last year of a physics degree, the senior undergraduates were invited to attend a lecture (on black holes) by one of the world's top astronomers. The man had a high-flying reputation—for his research, not for his speaking abilities. What a let-down. He was so bad as a speaker, that every time he turned his head to the blackboard, another swirl of students disappeared out the side door like planets down a black hole. And we had arrived with specific interest in the message.

As a presenter, you are the medium; you are most of your message.

I hope that's sobering to those who speak in monotones and officialese, or who have handed their authority over to PowerPoint. Their speech is a stone that slips into the pond without a ripple. Blank audience faces mask a desire for it to end, and polite applause expresses relief that it did. Within seconds there's no sign that it ever happened.

Instead, consider this.

> Effective presenters do not dispense information, they translate it.

When we dump knowledge on an audience and see blank faces, guess whose fault that is. It's ours. Whether or not the audience is dumb is completely irrelevant, because it's our job to translate our message into their language.

Some scientists protest. "The facts are the facts," they say. "Two plus two equals four, regardless of the audience." But that's not the point. It's not a presenter's job to give the information that two plus two equals four; rather to give an understanding that two plus two equals four. That's a huge difference.

To be a good translator you have to take into account not just the factual knowledge of your audience, but also their feelings about the topic. (See *What do they feel about the topic already?* p21) René Descartes got it wrong: his famous line, "I think, therefore I am," should have been written, "I feel, therefore I am". Human beings are driven by feelings not facts.

It is illogical to ignore feelings.

As for getting the best out of this book, you'll find many activities which suggest that you deliberately involve your own feelings and attitudes. If you do, you will significantly improve your chances of taking away real, lasting skills.

Making fear work for you

> "And Moses said, 'Please, Lord, don't send me. I was never a good speaker and I haven't become one since you began speaking to me." *Free translation of Exodus 4:10*

Asked to speak in public, Moses dug his toes into the sand and refused. The Almighty had not foreseen this eventuality and was irritated. But in this case fear of public speaking was greater than fear of His wrath, so He conceded defeat, put a hold on the bolt of lightning, and summoned Aaron to do the spokesman job.

Much of this book deals—either directly, or indirectly—with overcoming fear. If fear is one of your major concerns, look also at *How to overcome persistent symptoms of fear* p46, *For the truly terrified* p47, and the first performance key *Get engaged to the audience* p67.

Don't listen to anyone who lightly dismisses fear of public speaking as only in the mind. It's real, and although it starts in the mind, it can make your body do strange things, in front of other people, against your will.

At rest the human heart beats about 70 times per minute. While we are waiting to speak it can go as high as 190 a minute. That would lead to cardiac arrest if it was sustained, but it does head down after 30 seconds or so. There's only one other kind of stress reputed to have the same effect. Fear of death. In one study of 3,000 people in the U.S., the number of people who chose public speaking as their greatest fear exceeded the number who chose flying and the number who chose death *added together.* Which seems to suggests that some of us would rather drop dead at 35,000 feet than speak in public.

Fear comes from the mind and that's where we'll find the solution.

We really do have to tackle it, because very often our own thoughts multiply the problem far beyond the original level of fear. Scientists will tell you that when we see the audience looking at us, a message loop starts up in our brains. The upper brain thinks, 'Uh oh, I'm afraid'. It then sends—to the amygdala (the seat of our emotions) and ultimately to the whole nervous system—this message: *release the stress hormones!* So our heart rate climbs, our mouth dries, our hands and voices shake. Bad enough you might think, but the upper brain notices these results and says, 'Uh oh, now I'm truly terrified.' It promptly sends the next message: *release even more stress hormones!* And so on.[3] In other words, we are often afraid of being afraid.

In this book we'll be intervening in that vicious cycle, replacing it with something much more pleasurable for us and our audiences.

Why are so many of us so fearful?

Deep down, we know that an audience is the most efficient x-ray machine in the world. The moment we open our mouths in front of an audience, our protective veils will be instantly stripped away; the amount of personal authority we really have is going to be exposed. One archetypal nightmare has many of us walking out on stage only to discover that we're dressed for our original birthday.

You might have tried willpower. You might have tried logic, lecturing yourself in ringing tones like this: "Fear is not an option." Tried it? Doesn't work too well, does it? That's because we're often tackling subconscious forces. It's like trying to set the dogs onto a deep water shark. Even a mild case of nerves cannot be overcome by willing it to stop, because conscious willpower and fear of public speaking simply will not climb into the same boxing ring.

So fighting fear directly is not the answer.

Consider this. When you know that the true extent of your personal strength is going to be exposed, your subconscious senses danger. Imagine that you are a bus driver and your bus carries a capacity load of ancestors.

---

[3] *The Human Mind*, Robert Winston, 2004

They have agreed to keep quiet most of the time, but when danger looms they're allowed to get into the driver's seat with you. However, you wouldn't kick them out; it's a very sensible contract. Your ancient ancestors learned how to avoid becoming lunch for large carnivores. They developed surges of adrenaline that allowed for very fast, high-performance reactions. That's why you have signs of danger-readiness like dry mouth, wet armpits, cold sweaty palms, swallowing, increased heart rate and blood pressure.

Your ancestors bequeathed you a body that can be danger-ready in an instant, with an impulse known as 'fight or flight'. I'm not suggesting you express that impulse the same way—throwing the furniture at the audience or fleeing the room may not enhance your credibility—but it's time to recognize that you have been left a priceless gift.

Fear is not an enemy, it's a friend. Allow your friend to help you as your ancestors did: as a necessary tool for top performance. Then, quietly, your fear will become nervousness. Next, your nervousness will become a helpful and welcome surge of adrenaline.

I invite you to change your attitude to fear.

> Put your fear into gear. Use your nervous energy to make sure you fire on all cylinders.

See if you can pick this character: as a schoolboy he was shy and awkward in front of his classmates. He went on to distinguish himself in the Boer War and became an MP in the House of Commons. Even so, he was still so fearful of public speaking that in the middle of one of his addresses, he lisped, stuttered and collapsed in a heap on the floor. Yet, Winston Churchill went on to become better admired as a speaker than as a Prime Minister.

To win an encounter with *audiensaurus rex*, you don't have to be fearless.

And you don't have to be a natural. Most speakers are not born, they're self-made. Your current performance has nothing to do with your potential. Unless you believe otherwise of course. Henry Ford said this: "Whether you think you can, or whether you think you can't, you are probably right."

What are you thinking right now?

For more on handling fear, see *How to overcome persistent symptoms of fear* p46 and *For the truly terrified* p47.

Two life choices

It can hardly be a surprise that when you dig deeply into how to become an excellent speaker, you're going to find principles that will serve you far beyond the immediate target of speaking.

Here are two such principles. Those who live by them are usually well along the path to mastering their lives. Make these life choices your own.

LIFE CHOICE 1
Choose your attitude to any circumstance or event

"The great discovery of my generation is that a human being can alter his life by altering his attitudes." *William James*

You can't directly choose your feelings—they come from your history and deepest beliefs about who you are—but you can certainly choose your attitude. More: your choice can profoundly change the event itself because reality only has meaning as perceived reality. Your life is shaped much more by your reaction to an event than by the event itself.

A burglar trashes your house? You are not compelled to adopt any particular attitude or reaction. Your data-projector breaks down at the worst time? The audience hates your message? An interjector questions the marital status of your parents? You are entirely free to choose your response.

One of the worst excesses of pop psychology last century was the idea that to avoid becoming shrink fodder you should always 'be yourself'. Whatever you felt in one instant was 'you' and had to be acted out. So it became almost a duty to express those feelings which simply arrived, imposed themselves as 'you', and started directing your movie. A little matter was overlooked: that approach very quickly turned people into victims of their own feelings. They lost control.

Finally, the West is starting to understand that you can, quite deliberately, choose such life-altering, creative attitudes as optimism, contentment, courage and happiness. Take 1,000 people through the same event and 1,000 different paths will lead out the other side because at some level, conscious or otherwise, we do choose our response. Ten per cent of life is what happens to you, 90% is your attitude to what happens to you. Here's someone well qualified to say that we can, indeed, choose our attitude to any event.

> We who lived in concentration camps can remember the men who walked through the huts comforting others, giving away their last piece of bread. They offer sufficient proof that everything can be taken from a man but one last thing: the last of the human freedoms—to choose one's attitude in any given set of circumstances, to choose one's own way. *Victor Frankl, psychiatrist.*

If that attitude was possible under those circumstances, then we can certainly take better control of our response to much less dramatic events—such as presentations. Feel the strength of knowing that whatever happens in life, you can consciously choose your response.

LIFE CHOICE 2
Choose to be comfortable with the feelings of others.
Know that *all* feelings are beyond judgement.

This can seem bizarre until you realize the huge difference between feelings and the way feelings are expressed. There is also a huge difference between accepting feelings and accepting facts you disagree with. In each case, knowing the difference puts you in a position of great strength.

A city council CEO told me he was sitting at his office desk one day, when he heard a commotion. He put his head out of the door to see what was happening. And there, coming down the corridor, was an elderly man waving a stick and a rates demand. He was shouting abuse, staff were trying unsuccessfully to stop him, and he was heading for the CEO.

At this point, it might have been appropriate to threaten the man with calling the police if he didn't calm down. Instead, the CEO applied life choice 2.

"What's the matter?" he asked (tone neutral but concerned).

If anything the shouting got louder, and was accompanied by accusations and finger stabbing at the CEO's chest.

"Well," the CEO said, "if I thought that, I'd be angry too. Come and sit down and we'll see what we can sort out."

Not bad, is it? First there's the word 'angry', which shows that the CEO was willing to put a name to the elderly man's feeling, acknowledging it without judgement even though he would shortly be arguing against the man's facts or logic. Second—much, much more subtle—he simply chose to be comfortable in the face of the anger. The anger (not the way it was

14 How do I turn this book into real skills?

expressed) was completely natural given all the influences in that man's life up to that moment. The feeling was beyond judgement.

After the meeting, the old man emerged thinking of the CEO as a friend.

There's a special application of Life Choice 2 in *Accept feelings, argue facts* p108.

Passionate visualization:
how to programme your subconscious

> "Feelings are the great creator of the universe."
> *Hitchhikers Guide to the Galaxy*

> "Imagination rules the world." *Napoleon Bonaparte.*

Together, those two quotes declare the creative power of the human mind. It's a power we all use, all of the time. Some use it knowingly and take control of their lives. Many use it unknowingly, believing that life is controlling them.

Our beliefs have more power over our lives than a hurricane. They project from our subconscious, creating our lives around us as if they were a movie projector creating images on a full-surround screen. If you grow up believing (not just wishing strongly) that you will get into business, you will. If you grow up believing that nobody can get a job these days, you won't. We are a mass of countless beliefs, many overlapping, adding, subtracting, working for us, working against us. And we're only aware of a few of them. The power is not in the truth of the belief, but in the belief itself.

Do these beliefs sound familiar? "I'm no good at speaking in public." "I always get flustered in front of a group." "I'm useless without my notes." Many people are severely handicapped in life by the simple belief that they cannot speak easily in front of an audience. Few beliefs are so worthy of change.

And few are so easy to change.

> Your subconscious does not distinguish between real and unreal, it simply follows your instructions.

The following system can be applied to any goal. You can do, have or be anything you want. You will find the essence of this system at the centre of successful willpower, planned action, affirmations, visualizations, suggestion, hypnosis, meditation and prayer. And the more you throw your passions into it, the better the results.

Here are the three steps of passionate visualization. Here you'll use it to begin turning into a presenter with high confidence and personal authority. But it can be used for any goal. It is what highly motivated people do.

STEP ONE: Make the decision

Make the decision that you will become an excellent speaker.

Seems too obvious?

No it isn't. Don't underestimate this step. I've had people say to me, 'Okay, I understand this beliefs thing. I believe I could be a millionaire. But I haven't seen any of the money yet.' And I ask them, 'When did you make the decision to be one?' There's a world of difference between 'could be' and 'decision to be'. Countless goals fail for the lack of a clear, committed decision.

One morning, our managing director found himself in the lift with a young executive from another company in the same building. They introduced themselves.

"You people teach presentation skills, don't you?" she said.

"Yes, we do."

"I've avoided public speaking all my life," she said. "I can't do role plays, I just get incredibly nervous. But now I'm the manager in my branch and I'm expected to talk to clients regularly. It's my first presentation on Saturday. It's to 200 people. I need help."

She did the training with us. We then saw her speaking at the event she had feared, and she was very good indeed, a delight to watch and listen to. Then, a few weeks later, she and our MD met up, again by accident, again in the lift.

"You know, you guys have changed my life!" she exclaimed.

"Really?"

"I was so nervous about public speaking and now I'm taking every opportunity to do it. I just love it."

Well, our MD came into the office with a glow of satisfaction; but the glow faded just a little as he realized something. We had not changed her life—she had. Yes, we had an influence, but not the crucial one. The most vital ingredient was her clear decision that she was going to be an excellent speaker. That was the precursor that made our tips work.

I urge you to make the same clear decision.

Are you reading this book just to pick up a few tips? You'll get tips, of course, but if you really want them to work for you, *make the big decision*.

But don't make it until you've thought it out very carefully. Is it really what you want? Is the wording of your decision appropriate for you? Should you change the words 'excellent speaker' to 'confident speaker'? Should you change the word 'speaker' to 'communicator'? Work it out exactly before you commit.

Now, are you ready? Are you determined to make the goal real in your life?

All right, go ahead, make the decision.

Done it? How does it feel?

I'm not surprised. And your subconscious just turned over in bed and opened its eyes.

> "Success is not a matter of spontaneous combustion. You have to set yourself alight." *Abraham Lincoln*

STEP TWO: Visualize passionately

Vividly imagine yourself giving an excellent presentation and as you do so *wallow* in the strongest possible feelings of satisfaction, pleasure and personal strength.

There's an old saying: what man can conceive, he can achieve. But it should be said like this: what man can passionately conceive, he will certainly achieve.

Passion is the magic ingredient. Visualization is well known, but passionate visualization is not—which is extraordinary because passion is the catalyst that makes the subconscious bound out of bed and start working for you. Only with focused passion can your imagination start pushing reality into the shape you want.

try this... Take the phone off the hook, sedate the children and find a quiet spot. Play music that inspires you. Picture yourself standing in front of a likely audience. Picture the setting. Picture the walls, with hangings, the curtains, the floor. What's the texture of the carpet? What's the design? Picture the audience, with all the texture and weave and colour of their clothes. Now put expressions on their faces. They're looking at you and listening to your words with considerable interest. You know you're performing well.

Feel the warm glow of satisfaction.

You recognize some faces of people you know. Give them names. You're performing so effectively, with such confidence and authority that many have small grins of enjoyment. Others are giving those almost imperceptible nods that indicate understanding and appreciation. What you're saying is sinking in.

Feel the surge of pleasure.

Think ahead. Hear in your mind the words of relatives, friends, colleagues, bosses when they say to you, "Well done." "Good job." "Enjoyed that." Your buzz of satisfaction becomes an inner thrill of enjoyment. You have power to influence people.

Feel the strength in you. You didn't realize how good this could be!

Finally, finish with a flourish and leave with applause ringing in your ears. You have entertained them, persuaded them, convinced them, inspired them. You have the power to influence people.

You *feel* wonderful.

STEP THREE: Act consistently with the goal

Make all your subsequent actions consistent with the goal of becoming an excellent presenter. The goal is inevitable; every step takes you towards it.

Are you one who says, 'Don't pick me.'? When you have to go forward to speak, do you say, 'Oh, well, I'd better get it over with.'? When you get out there, do you say, 'I'm not much of a public speaker, so I'll make this short.'? You may not realize just how much such thoughts, words and actions have been undermining you as a self-fulfilling prophecy.

The old myth was that you were allotted a certain number of brain cells not long after B day and they steadily died off and couldn't be replaced. But that's all it was—a myth.

Modern neuroscience accepts that the brain is a living, changing organism[4]. The principle agent of change is you. Your *thoughts* alter the physical and chemical structure of your brain, weakening or strengthening the neural networks associated with those thoughts. Every thought makes a subtle change. Repeated thoughts make bigger changes. Frequently repeated passionate thoughts significantly alter the structure of the brain and make deep inroads into your subconscious which goes right on obeying you.

Two and a half thousand years ago, the Buddha said, "All that we are is the result of what we have thought. The mind is everything. What we think, we become."

What have you been thinking?

More to the point: what have you been feeling? Thoughts are feelings without the juice. The potency of a feeling is many times the potency of a thought.

---

[4] Source, *The Human Mind*, Robert Winston, 2004

Maybe it's time to take hold of your own reins. Imagine—after you've done the first two steps—that you become one who says things like, "Sure, I'll do the presentation." And "I enjoy speaking." And "Have you got a speaker for Monday? I want to do it." Now there's an attractive self-fulfilling prophecy to invite home to dinner.

Are you ready to take control of your own mind? Are you ready to think big about your potential as a speaker? Are you ready to entertain the idea that you could feel confidence and pleasure when you speak?

Put your IQ in second place

Leaning how to become a good presenter, your ability to think will be handy, but it won't be enough on its own. If you want real skills and lasting confidence, you will have to give first place to your passions. How badly do you want to overcome fear and become confident and authoritative in front of other people? If you really want that, then I urge you to throw heart and soul into the activities ahead—many of which deliberately involve your feelings and other people.

High quality research (an average of several studies) has found that:

>...we retain 10% of what we read.
>...we retain 70% of what we talk over with others.
>...we retain 80% of what we use and do.

(Association of Research Libraries)

>"We ask ourselves, "Who am I to be brilliant, gorgeous, talented, fabulous?" Actually, who are you not to be? Your playing small does not serve the world.
>
>...As we let our own light shine, we unconsciously give other people permission to do the same. As we are liberated from our own fear, our presence automatically liberates others."
>
>*Marianne Williamson*

 # How do I prepare?

Begin the process of winning your audience
before you see them

Good preparation is like assembling a bicycle. It needs both wheels if you expect to ride on it. Obvious. So why do so many presenters produce the speech equivalent of a bicycle with a missing wheel?

Wheel number one is the message. If it's expressed fluently and enthusiastically, then that's the tyre pumped up. Presenters understand that.

Wheel number two? Make the message connect to the audience. Remember that first personal authority: the ability to connect. Much of it will be in your manner and style on the day, but a great deal of it starts with your preparation. To get your second wheel on and pumped you'll prepare to generate these thoughts in your audience: *This content is relevant to me. This presenter knows where I'm coming from. I trust her. She respects me and I respect her.*

This chapter shows how to assemble your bicycle with both wheels.

Ask the how/what/where questions

If you don't know the answers to these questions, you may need to find out:

How long do I speak?
Little planning is possible if you don't know. If you're calling the shots, tell the organizer what you anticipate.

Is food involved?
Imagine. You eat a four course dinner on the way, then discover a five course dinner at the function, with you at the head table.

Are there any curtains?
Many a presentation has foundered at the start gun because nobody thought to check until the presenter turned up with the data-show. Also, will the sun light up the translucent curtains?

What layout do you want?
Boardroom? U-shape? The U-shape encourages good audience interaction. For medium sized audiences, the best all-purpose arrangement is called the

'chevron' after an NCO's stripes: rows angled about 20 degrees so everyone faces slightly inwards. For small meetings involving paperwork, my favourite is the plain boardroom style.

What are the alcohol arrangements?
If the audience is going to be lubricated you had better modify your speech on parallels between Eastern religious thought and recent discoveries in quantum physics.

What's the audience going to be wearing?
That's how you find out what you'll wear. As a general rule, dress the same or slightly better than the audience; what's at stake here is how the audience perceives your respect for them.

What audio-visual aids are available? Will you have technical back-up?
Will you need time to rehearse with the technician?

What else will the audience be getting?
Changes may be necessary if your post-modernist perspective on Icelandic syntax comes right after the belly dancing. Also, what is this audience used to? Light-hearted banter or highbrow intellectualism? Who is speaking immediately before you and what are their topics?

What is the official title for your speech or presentation?
That's not trivial. Suppose you're an expert in how to stop sheep-dog viruses destroying farmers' livelihoods. But someone has given your talk the title 'A discussion on farm animals and micro-organisms.' You may find no-one there to listen.

Ask the crunch audience questions

This is where audience connection starts in earnest. The whole scope of your preparation and structure, the tone you adopt and the language you use will be affected by the answers.

What kind of people will be there?
What professions? What interests? What mix of genders? Will the audience individuals know each other? Are they all members of the same group? The answers can tell you a lot about the atmosphere you can expect.

What do they know about the topic already?
Are they all armed with the latest knowledge? Do they know nothing about it? Is there a mixture? Very often there's a mixture of expertise and you'll have to take that into account, so as not to risk being insulting to one part of

your audience and boring to another. You need to know what level of jargon is acceptable. The fine details of printed circuit boards may be fascinating to electronics engineers, but would cause an audience of electronics salesmen to reach for anxiety pills.

Will there be experts in the audience?
How many are likely to know more about the topic, or parts of it, than you? If the answer is yes, see *When there's an expert in the audience*, p121.

Why will the audience be there; what do they expect from you?
Are they there willingly? Do they have a passing level of interest already or will they be there under orders?

And above all, this.

What do they feel about the topic already?
Even if you were to leave out every other question, don't ignore this one. Not knowing the answer can lead to nightmarish speaking disasters. Knowing it will lead you into one of the most powerful components of persuasion: pre-empting objections and concerns. (For details see p27)

Ask these subsidiary questions. How strong are the feelings involved? Are they entrenched? Is the audience divided? If so, what proportion feel one way? What proportion the other? How many are undecided? Why do they have the feelings they do? If you're asking someone else for these answers, take nothing as gospel. For hot issues, it's possible that no one can give you an unbiased picture.

And what questions are they likely to ask you? What are the *worst* questions they could ask you? What emotions could they throw at you? Toughest of all—what questions and concerns could be on the mind of an audience too polite to interrupt? If you don't know, those unacknowledged concerns may silently sabotage your presentation.

Suppose, for example, you're planning to tell a well-behaved audience (too polite to interrupt) about a wonderful new computer system. What you don't know is that last time they got lumbered with a new computer system, half of them were treated for paranoia and the rest applied for early retirement. Do you think knowing that in advance might affect your preparation?

Be informed about, open to, and comfortable with audience feelings about your topic. Ignore them at your peril.

The four-step, all-purpose preparation (the city model)

> "It usually takes me more than three weeks to prepare a good impromptu speech." *Mark Twain.*

Nice humour. The reality is that good preparation can be swift and easy, as long as you follow a few simple rules. And the process should be reassuring, because feeling good about a presentation starts with feeling well prepared. The city model method will handle virtually all types of presentation. (For exceptions, see *How do I handle formal or special occasions* p125.)

What you'll need: an ordinary black pen and a packet of coloured felt pens, a blank sheet of paper (to be your brainstorm page), a copy of the presentation notes form (you can enlarge the blank form on page 51), and research sources for factual content.

Here are the terms we'll use:

The *city-view* is an overview that tells the audience your real purpose with them.

A *suburb* is a label you give to any section of your presentation.

A *street* is any detail.

How do I prepare? 23

A *signpost* tells the audience where you are in your presentation.

The order of preparation is not the same as the order of delivery to the audience. To put the entire preparation method in perspective, you might like to glance ahead at the summary on page 39.

STEP 1 — WRITE THE CITY-VIEW SENTENCE

This is the most crucial part of the preparation and the core of your whole presentation. It's where you get to the point. It's where you come right out with it. It's where you tell them why you're really there. And, believe it or not, most presenters do not tell their audiences why they're really there. Here's how to avoid that mistake.

- Ask yourself: "What do I want my audience to think, feel or do as a result of this presentation?"

- Use this city-view generator to write the sentence:

CITY-VIEW GENERATOR

I want to…	convince you that… show you that/why/how… demonstrate that/how… tell you how… outline the…	(statement)
A	B	C

A. The words 'I want' acknowledge that it's *you* on the line, not your topic. You can say, "I'm going to…" but be careful—if you follow it with "…convince you…' then you had better have a twinkle in your eye when you say it, or the audience will take you as arrogant—surely the last thing you want.

B. If the topic is suitable, then the word 'that', gives you a high authority city-view sentence that puts you and your opinions on the front line. *I want to show you that the new schedule will reduce our costs.* Likewise, the word 'convince' increases your impact. It takes nerve to use them both, but when you do, you'll get an assertive, authoritative sentence which makes people sit up and take notice. *I want to convince you that if we don't lower our rates we will lose our best customers.* Which brings me to the main point.

Powerful presenters take a position, adopt a stance.
They do not try to be (or pretend to be) objective.

Of course many topics just don't suit high impact statements. For example, it's often important to convey facts without your opinion, in which case you would not use either 'that' or 'convince'. *I want to outline the new structure of the HR department.* Or, *I want to outline the facts so you can make up your own minds where to go from here.* However, be careful. Many presenters—wanting to play safe and avoid criticism—tell themselves that objectivity is a virtue and eliminate their own opinions when that is exactly what the audience needs.

Warning! Have you noticed that the city-view generator doesn't contain the word 'about'? That's because "I want to talk about..." tells the audience that you're going to have a safe, detached discussion in which you personally are not on the line. Even worse is the stuffy phrase, "My topic is...", which has the same effect as administering a powerful sedative to your audience.

"I'm going to talk about..." BORING!

"My topic is..." BORING!

C. The reason you're there. Only you will know that, but consider this:

Where possible,
lock the topic to the audience with the word 'you'.

I want to show you how higher taxes benefit you in the long run works much better than *I want to show you that higher taxes is a good thing*. However it isn't always possible or appropriate. Many audiences—especially technical, scientific and medical—are there only to increase their general knowledge and you would not expect them to think, feel or do anything as a result of your presentation.

So that's the city-view sentence—telling the audience why you're really there.

There's a lot in that word 'really'. I was once asked to help a few scientists with a practice run for a national seminar that would include politicians and fund managers in the audience. To call the seminar important would be an understatement. For the practice session one scientist stood up front and I sat with half a dozen of his fellow specialists. I'll call him Dave. On a highly controversial subject, guaranteed to rouse passions, he started like this (and notice the use of the word 'about...').

"Good morning everyone. I want to talk about 1080 poison and the residual effects in animal cells."

You might say that was fair enough—a clear description of the topic. And Dave was certainly articulate and skilled with visual aids. Even so, after 10 minutes I was lost, and the expressions of his fellow specialists indicated that they were struggling too.

"Are you wanting to convince us of anything?" I asked.

"Well, yes," Dave said, surprised. He flapped his hand at the data as if it was self-explanatory. "I want to convince you that 1080 poison is still the only viable option."

Ahah. Did you pick the word 'that'? The expressions on the faces of his colleagues cleared. To a man and woman they all nodded. Now they had a perspective. Now he was coming right out with it. Now they knew why he was really there.

(NOTE: in fact there were two major mistakes in that opening of his. On this hot topic he ignored the passions that politicians and fund managers would bring into the room. If you like, glance ahead to *Acknowledge the predominant mood*, p33; but for now I'm going to stay strictly with the order of preparation—different from the order of delivery.)

try this... Find a city-view sentence for your own topic. Using your black pen and the city-view generator, write your own sentence in the centre of your blank sheet of paper (which now becomes the brainstorm page).

So your brainstorm page should start out looking like this.

CHECK: Does your city-view sentence tell the audience why you're really there? Does it openly convey your agenda? Does it (where possible) tell the audience how you want them to think, feel or act as a result of your presentation? And does it (where possible) indicate the relevance of your topic to the audience?

If so, you now have the core of your presentation. The rest will be fleshed out around it—starting with the brainstorm.

BRAINSTORM AND RESEARCH

Here's a suggestion: read right through Step 2 before you do anything.

Brainstorming (some call it mind-mapping) is a crucial few minutes in the development of a presentation or speech. Many neglect it and start writing or structuring immediately—a mistake, because it ignores the value of lateral thinking. In step two, deliberately avoid structuring. Also, if you can, avoid lists, sets and subsets. Just let the ideas pour out and edit later.

A typical brainstorm page looks like the diagram on page 29: single words or phrases—just enough to remind you of the idea. As you jot things down, remember the second wheel: relate your content to the audience.

Prepare to broadcast on WIIFM

You haven't heard of this radio station? But every single member of your audience is an avid listener. Here it is: *What's In It For Me?* Prepare to make your content specifically relevant to the audience in a way that talks to the audience. Very often that will mean using the word 'you'. *Your computers will handle this stuff, but you'll find them pretty sluggish.* Audiences hearing that word 'you' do not doze off.

So as you jot things down, keep these questions in mind: "What can I add to make my material relevant to this audience?" Also "What can I add to take into account what the audience feels about the topic?"

Which brings me to a device that will guarantee you a huge advantage. The device is not well known, but once you discover its brilliance, you'll always use it. It's called pre-empting objections.

Pre-empt objections and concerns

Do yourself a huge favour…

Prepare to take it to the audience
before they take it to you.

Dealing with objections and concerns before they are raised by the audience is one of the most successful of all ways to convince and persuade. It's very good psychology because even the most sceptical audience says to itself, "This presenter understands where I'm coming from." That's also a wonderful way to take the steam out of a difficult audience.

- Think of all the objections, concerns and related feelings the audience might have about your topic. Mentally, become them.

- For each item, ask, "How could this objection or concern be wrong?" If it's wrong, jot down (on the brainstorm page) a reminder of your reply. If it's not wrong, jot down an acknowledgement—it's still good psychology to bring it up yourself. It's not a defeat. It just says that you've considered the whole picture.

    Note: the word 'wrong' refers to an apparent fact or conclusion that arises from a feeling. Argue facts and conclusions assertively, but never judge the feeling itself. (See *Accept feelings, argue facts* p108)

Then you may need to make the following choice about the answers.
EITHER
Prepare to verbalize it directly. For example, if you anticipate the objection "This has got nothing to do with me", you might jot down *relevance*, and in the speech itself say, "You may be wondering what this has to do with you…" Or, if you anticipate a cost objection, you might jot down *cost* and say, "Some of you are concerned about the cost. Yes, this will be expensive. And it will be worth it because…." Notice how the word 'you' is used?

Talking directly to the audience about their concerns is very strong and very persuasive. It's a tool used by effective leaders.
OR:
Prepare to deal with it indirectly. If you anticipate the usually unspoken concern, "Can I trust this person?" (meaning you), you might jot down *contract safeguards* and talk about those without using the word trust.

Prepare specific illustrations, metaphors, word pictures and stories

Why? Because this is how core messages really sink in. However worthy, an unsupported general statement has little inherent impact; it's your code for what's important to you and audiences don't feel the importance just by listening to your code. Attach something specific.

> Not just "This model is structurally sound", but also, "We laid a concrete slab on it—642kg—and there was no damage" and also, "You could run an elephant over it". (So on your brainstorm page you might jot down *Concrete, 642kg, Elephant.*)

Of course making your general statement with passion does help, but you still need the illustrations. Don't hesitate to use specific names, times, dates, colours, textures.

> Not just "We need to change procedures at reception" but also, "Just last week a young woman with a baby and a toddler had to wait 20 minutes in a reception queue to make a complaint about the length of our queues." (Jot down *Customer 20 mins.*)

One part of us never grows up. We love stories. The moment you start telling a story, you'll see an approving shift in the expressions in your audience. The more specific and detailed the better. Paint pictures with your words.

> Not just "Cutting prices now would send the wrong signal to our established customers" but also, "It will be like getting down on our knees and begging." (Jot down *Wrong signal, On knees*)

> "Imagine my problem. There I was in an old fashioned stairwell, carved banister, red carpet, moth holes, and I was just..." (Jot down *Stairwell*)

Prepare to surprise them

Be unpredictable. Not just in your material, but in the way your express it.

Don't tell them what they know already. Instead, jot down ideas which acknowledge what they know, and tell them what they don't.

"As you may know, the schedule is about to change. Be careful with Day Two." (Jot down *Know change, careful day 2*)

Prepare contrasts, which stimulate feelings in the audience.

"This is not a drain on our resources, but an investment in the long term vitality of this firm." (Jot down *not a drain, is investment*)

Do your research

Why is this last in the brainstorm? Because everything up to this point has been driven by how the audience is going to relate to the topic. Be audience-centred rather than fact-driven. That's how you become good at persuading and convincing.

So do your normal research, adding to or changing your brainstorm page as you go: facts and figures, supporting quotes, graphs and relevant quotes. You may need a phone call or two to research the audience.

try this... Brainstorm your own topic. Look at your city-view sentence. Tell yourself the audience wants you to be interesting, entertaining, and memorable. Now write your ideas all over the brainstorm page, twisting the page to a new angle for each idea. Don't censor or structure. Don't pause. Your mind is never empty. Fly through as many ideas as you can for at least five minutes. Think of yourself as an open tap for ideas.

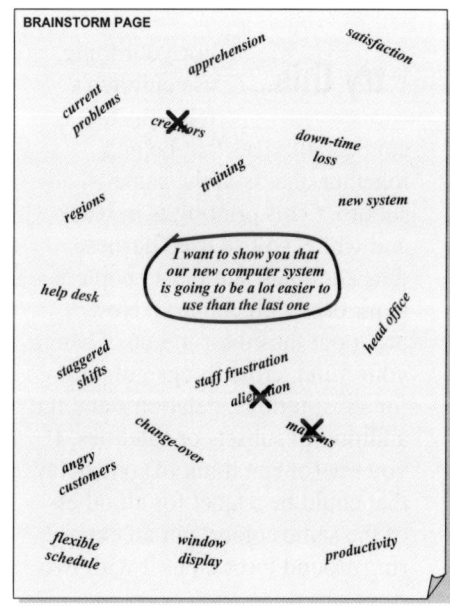

Here's a summary guide on what to include.

- Jot down ways to broadcast on WIIFM (p26). Relating it to the audience boosts impact.

30 How do I prepare?

- Jot down ways to pre-empt objections, concerns, related questions. What are the worst questions they could ask you? What are their likely unspoken objections—those that silently undermine the effectiveness of your presentation?
- Jot down illustrations, metaphors and word pictures. Anecdotes? Illustrative recent events? Something a client has said?
- Jot down things that will surprise them.
- As a final check, complete the loop. Go back to your city-view sentence. Do you now want to modify it? Look back through your jottings and ask yourself, Is this point relevant to my city-view? If the answer is no, be ruthless.

STEP 3 CONNECT YOUR IDEAS

 For your topic, use children's felt pens to connect all ideas that belong together, that is in the same suburb. (This printing is in black and white, so I've used dashes, dots and lines, but most people work best with colours). Now bring out the editor in you. Change your mind, cross things out, allow for substitutions, deletions, and the addition of subsets or satellites. If you see (or can think of) one detail that could be a label for all others of the same colour, put an extra ring around it (or enter it with two rings).

My example has three suburbs. The human mind responds well to

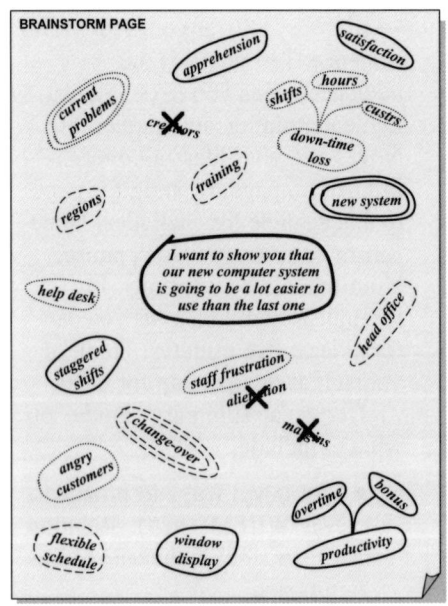

that number, but it could easily be two or four, or even one for a very simple talk. If you get to larger numbers, five and up, that's more difficult for audiences to take in. See if you can combine some of them.

If you don't care for colours, or dots and dashes, get a pair of scissors, isolate every detail and connect your ideas by shuffling bits of paper into columns that look like the presentation notes form in Step 4.

STEP 4 ORGANISE YOUR IDEAS

try this... *Transfer all your information* to the presentation notes form as below. Modify as you go. Give each column of streets a suburb name. There's a blank template at the end of this chapter you can photocopy and enlarge.

try this... *Enter your opening spotlight.*
The average audience takes less than ten seconds to decide if you're going to be worth listening to. Granville Toogood in *The Articulate Executive* puts it at eight seconds. A documentary study by a group of British psychologists found that interviewers listening to job applicants had made up their minds irreversibly within five seconds. The spotlight is worth very careful thought. It can come from your brainstorm page, or it can be something new.

It comes right after the greeting and just before the city-view.

It's a sentence (or more) that reaches out to the audience, grabs it by the scruff of its collective shirt and says, "Get this. What follows is going to be interesting and relevant to you!"

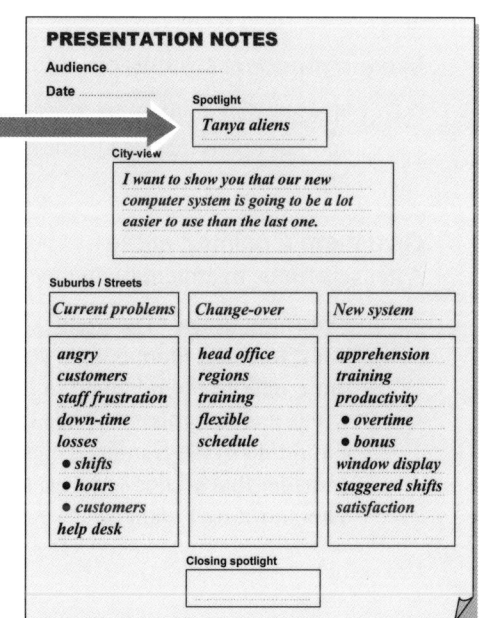

There are two ways to create an opening spotlight:

EITHER: Establish a common interest with the audience
There are several standard ways to do it.

Tell an anecdote
A small, relevant story. It could be humorous, but never tell an unrelated joke which may raise a laugh, but ends in a let-down. Tradition has it that you tell a joke to relax the audience. Tradition is wrong; usually the one who needs to relax is the speaker. Get detailed. Get personal. Paint pictures with your words. And make sure the link with your speech is clear.

> "Last Tuesday, Sue and I went to see *Love Story*... yes in the back row... We were in the middle of the most passionate moment... no, not our own... when some idiot up front let off an alarm clock. Well... (link to city-view) I have to tell you that the arrival of competition is the alarm clock for everyone in this room. (city-view) This afternoon I want to..."

Ask a pointed question

> "How often have you stopped in the middle of some slavery for your boss and said, 'There has to be something better than this!'? Well there is. Today I want to..."

Make a personal statement

> "Ladies and gentlemen. Twenty years ago, I resolved not to touch another cigarette if it killed me. I haven't and it hasn't. This morning I want to..."

Give them a pointed quote
After scurrilous treatment by the media:

> "Morning, folks. 'The greatest happiness is to vanquish your enemies, to chase them before you, to rob them of their wealth, to see those dear to them bathed in tears, to clasp to your bosom their wives and daughters.' That's Genghis Khan's advice on what we should do to the Sunday Telegraph. But I suspect the media would consider that a knee jerk reaction, so we need to find another way. This morning I want to..."

Make a hard-hitting statement

> "Morning everyone. I have to tell you that if we do not reach agreement tonight, then in six months this branch... will... no longer... exist!"

Give them a stunt

At a weight-watchers convention, a motivation speech might begin with:

> "Anne? Anne Higgins? Ah, there you are..." You leave the stage and head for Anne. (Anne has made significant weight loss and agreed to this). You sweep her off her feet and hold her high.

OR: Acknowledge the predominant audience mood

Take careful note of this one, especially if you anticipate a difficult audience. It's not showmanship at all—it's quite simply one of the most powerful elements you can put into a presentation, winning the respect of even the most challenging audience.

Will your audience have a major negative feeling about your topic? If the answer is yes, you may *have* to acknowledge it as your spotlight.

> (Spotlight) "I know that many of you feel badly about what's happened, and some of you are concerned about your working conditions. (City-view) So, this morning, I want to outline..."

This method alarms some inexperienced presenters. They argue that it invites trouble. In practice, it defuses trouble, because it shows that you know 'where the audience is coming from'. Yes, you may trigger a small vocal outburst, but it will fade quickly, replaced by the urge to listen to you.

try this... *Enter your closing spotlight*

Lord Mancroft once said, "A speech is like a love affair. Any fool can start it, but to end it requires considerable skill." But it's easier than Mancroft thought, especially if you use more of the kind of material you put in the opening spotlight. Your ending could be a quote, a call to action, or a re-emphasis of the main points.

Above all, it must be delivered strongly. Audiences remember endings well, so take advantage of it. End with increased energy, and a tone that indicates you have just completed something important. An example: "And finally, as Oscar Wilde put it: 'When I was young I thought money was the most important thing in life; now I am old, I know that it is.' Now let's go out and... *get... wealthy*!"

Incidentally, Oscar Wilde produced an exit line on his own deathbed. He said, "Either this wallpaper goes, or I do."

Rehearse the order of delivery

Introduction spotlight, city-view, suburbs preview.
Main body suburb 1, suburb 2, suburb 3, etc.
Conclusion suburbs review, city-view review, closing spotlight.

Tell them what you're going to tell them,
tell them,
then tell them what you told them.

That saying has been around for decades with good reason. It works. Audiences appreciate it and they understand the content better.

INTRODUCTION (Telling them what you're going to tell them.)
Rehearse your own introduction from your presentation notes.

Opening spotlight →	"Afternoon everyone. Michelle Robbins tells me her worried three-year-old daughter Tanya confronted her in the garden last night and demanded to know if computers were for fighting aliens... which describes our situation, doesn't it? Most of us feel as if we're fighting an alien culture."
(...and link)	
City-view →	"This morning I want to show you that the new computer system is going to be much easier to use and much more efficient than the one we've had."
Suburbs *pre*view → (formal presentations only. Very brief—with pauses between)	"We'll look at our current problems... (pause)... we'll look at the change-over timetable (pause)... and we'll look at what we can expect from the new system."

Time & questions? (if necessary) ➔	"We should be finished by lunch time... Do ask questions as we go..."

Once you get used to this system, you'll find you can deliver a stirring introduction with nothing more than five minutes notice and a few words scribbled on the presentation notes form.

MAIN BODY (Telling them.)

suburb one ➔	"First then, the current problems..."
suburb two ➔	"Now, the change-over timetable..."
suburb three (etc) ➔	"All right, that's the timetable. Now let's look at what we can expect from the new system..."

CONCLUSION (Telling them what you told them.)

Suburbs review ➔ (formal presentations only)	"We've seen how disastrous the old system has been... (pause) we've seen we'll be in for a difficult change-over... (pause)... but we've also seen how much we've got to gain once this is in place."
City-view review ➔	"So, I'm asking you to accept that the new system is not only going to increase our efficiency, it's going to transform working conditions for all of us."
Closing spotlight ➔	"Young Tanya Robbins was probably relieved to discover that she didn't have to fight aliens. The new computer system looks very promising, and I believe we'll all feel something of that same relief. Thank you."

Don't write prompt notes to be hand-held

Hand-held prompt cards are very difficult to use naturally. For example, there's no such thing as an unobtrusive glance at your cards. It's all too obvious and usually looks like an awkward compromise. Far better are obvious prompt notes left on a nearby surface. An enlargement of the presentation notes form on page 51 is ideal. When you need a reminder,

36 How do I prepare?

you'll make an open movement to it, usually in silence, re-engaging with the audience before you speak again. (Also see p58)

If you must read out a fully written speech

"He who reads speech talks to own navel." *Anon.*

That's a little harsh on world-class orators—John F Kennedy, Winston Churchill and Nelson Mandela are good examples—who stir the emotions of a large crowd and make them forget that every word is coming right off the notes. But if you're not intending to be an orator, reading a speech usually means settling for second best. That's because no matter how good your preparation you will find it much more difficult to engage the audience, automatically sacrificing rapport. That's quite a sacrifice.

However, sometimes there's no choice. You're lumbered with someone else's speech, or tight legal issues make spontaneity risky, or there are journalists in the audience with pens poised to attack. If so:

On each page

- Use a large font. Don't write in upper case which is hard to read.

- Make every sentence a separate paragraph and don't break any sentence with a page change.

- Use 1.5 line-spacing with an extra line before the paragraph. Indent each first line.

- Put page numbers in every corner. Dropping your notes then taking too long to sort them out can make for a comedy act with you as the main attraction.

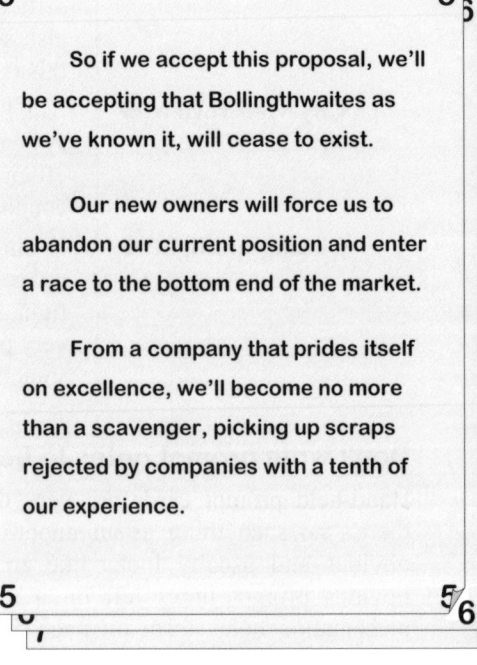

Here's a good compromise, which allows for spontaneity, but still gives you the security of a written speech.

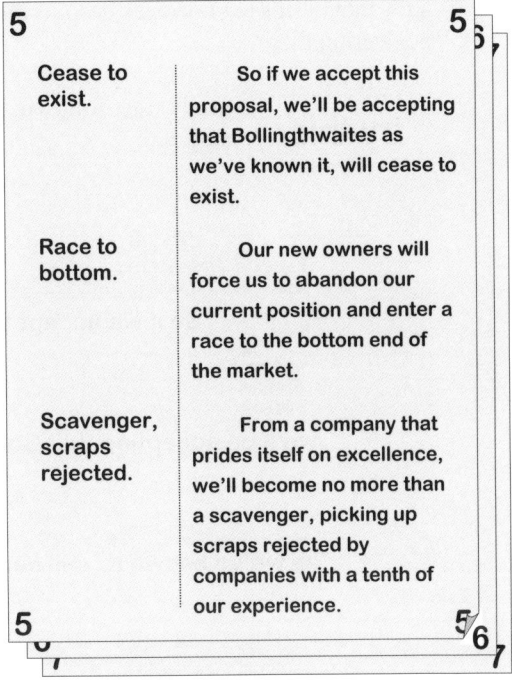

Now boost your audience rapport by reading so that you don't seem to be reading. (This method assumes a sizeable audience. It would look too ponderous for a small working meeting.)

- Take half a step back so that your eyes don't have to drop too much to look at your notes.

- In silence scan the first phrase of the sentence, look up.

- Engage the eyes of the audience and speak the first phrase.

- Look down as you read out the middle section of the sentence and scan ahead to the last phrase.

- Look up and engage the audience to speak the last phrase. That's more than just look in the direction of the audience, that's engage their eyes. It takes at least another quarter of a second.

- Repeat for next sentence.

Yes, they will see your eyes drop to the page, but it will not seem as if you're neglecting them.

try this... Study the following example, then try it on your own material:

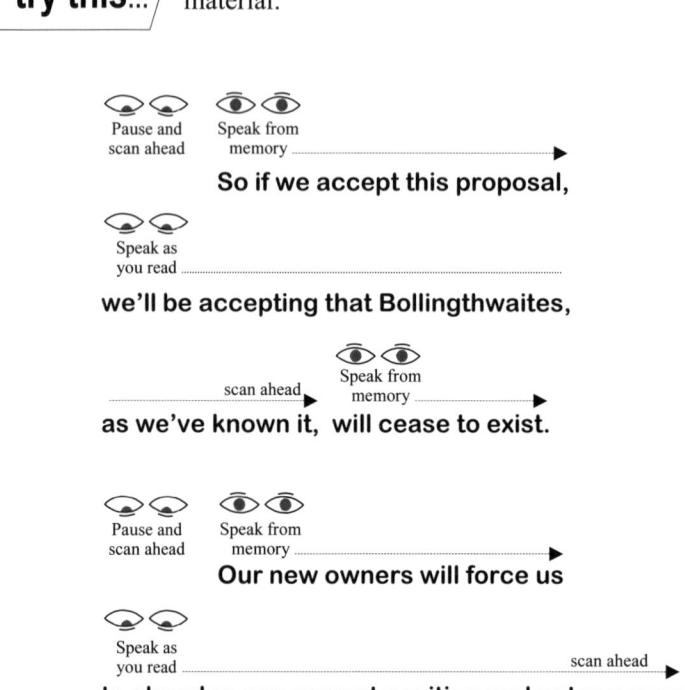

It works very well. With practice, you'll look as if your attention is more on people than on paper. Most of us do need that practice because the method reverses our normal impulse to start uttering the words as soon as we start reading the beginning of the sentence. That impulse comes from fear of silence; we think that if we're silent the audience will assume we've forgotten our words or lost control. In practice, effective presenters often make deliberate use of silence. See *The power of silence* p87)

Now, let's put the entire preparation together.

Summary

Prepare in this order:

 Write the city-view sentence
Use the city-view generator to write your bottom-line purpose with the audience.

 Brainstorm & research
Brainstorm first, then add more with normal factual research.

 Connect your ideas
Connect ideas using coloured pens.

 Organize your ideas
Transfer ideas onto the presentation notes form.
Give each column a suburb heading.
Add opening and closing spotlights.

Deliver from the presentation notes in this order:

	LONGER FORMAL SPEECHES	SHORTER INFORMAL SPEECHES
Introduction	opening spotlight city-view suburbs *pre*view duration & questions?	opening spotlight city-view

Main body	suburb & streets
	  suburb & streets
	    suburb & streets
		streets

Conclusion	suburbs *re*view city-view *re*view closing spotlight	city-view *re*view closing spotlight

How to prepare for a difficult audience

The good news is that it's no different from what you have just been practising. Even so, you'll want to focus especially on some parts of the method. Pay special attention to:

- *The spotlight: acknowledging the audience mood, feeling, or major objection.* Your tough audience will not listen to your facts until they hear you acknowledge their feelings and concerns. It doesn't have to be lengthy (sometimes just a phrase will do it), but it does have to be there. And remember—acknowledging is completely different from 'agreeing with'.

- *The city-view.* Give special attention to telling the audience directly and openly what you want to achieve by speaking to them. The more difficult the audience, the more important this is and the more they will quietly respect you (often at the same time as disagreeing with you). The opposite is true of presenters who skirt around the point—that simply invites disrespect and trouble. Audiences reserve a special place in hell for presenters who dodge the issue.

- *Pre-empting their objections, concerns & related questions.* Take it to them before they take it to you. Time spent working out those objections and concerns in advance is time invested in your control and authority.

- *Broadcasting on WIIFM.* The audience will feel that you are connected to them, not just speaking at them. Prepare to use the word 'you'.

In the hours before

Rehearse

Winston Churchill's valet was passing his bathroom one night, when he heard the sound of Churchill's voice above the sound of splashing in the bathtub.

"Were you speaking to me, Sir?" the valet called out.

"No," Churchill snapped, annoyed at the interruption, "I was addressing the House of Commons."

Whatever rehearsal method you use, do your first the day before and do it as close as you can to going to sleep. At night your subconscious goes to work on adrenaline-producing problems, using resources you didn't even know you had. Rehearse again in the morning and you'll find a marked improvement.

Act your rehearsal, don't just say it. Act it with all the enthusiasm and emphasis you can muster, because that makes it sink in.

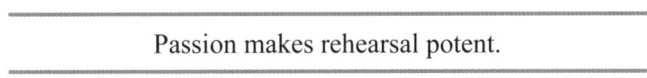

Passion makes rehearsal potent.

- Act it in front of a mirror. Try to persuade your reflected self.
- Pace around in a room, talking to your imagined audience.
- Enlist the help of a friend or colleague as a trial audience. Again, treat it as a performance, not just rehearsal of verbal content.

Dress for the part

I once saw a speech entirely ruined by the clothes of the presenter. At first sight there wasn't much difference between his clothes and ours. Most of us were in good jeans, open necked shirts and casual shoes. He was in faded jeans held up with string, a T shirt, and thongs, in each case only one grade down on what we wore. And yet the focus of the audience was so drawn to his attire, his message was lost. His intention, I guessed, was to say to his audience, *I am not a stuffed shirt like those who normally give speeches*. At the intellectual level, they got that message. But at the visceral level they got entirely another, which said, *I do not respect you*.

If possible, dress the same or slightly better than your audience, but never below your normal range.

'Never below your normal range' because your audience will sense that it just isn't you. I once did a television feature on a bikie gang. Had I dressed the same or slightly better than the bikies I would have been seen as false and—rightly—earned their contempt. I stayed in jacket and tie. They stayed in filthy jeans and tee shirts. We communicated without any problems.

Some extra points.

- *Comfort*. Make sure the clothing is easy to wear.
- *Colour*. Wear something with a bright colour or two to draw audience eyes. For men in conservative suits, the only option is a bright tie.

- *Pockets*. Bulging pockets are a distraction for the audience. Remove coins and keys.

- *Shoes*. If the shoes can be shined, shine them. Under every stone, you'll find consultants with opinions on what you should wear in business. A point they'll all agree on is that shoes that can shine, must.

- *Hair*. Keep hair off the forehead, upper cheeks and lips. The visual signals from the face have importance way out of proportion to those from the rest of the body.

Women need to be especially careful. In spite of the march of gender equality, men can get away with poor dress sense and still be listened to. Women cannot. And the most demanding audience for a poorly dressed woman is women.

Put Dutch courage back in the bottle

I have seen interesting exceptions, but they are rare. Usually Dutch courage works only in the mind of the presenter. Shakespeare said, "Drink provokes the desire but it takes away the performance," though he may not have had public speaking in mind at the time.

Arrive early

If you arrive right on show-time assuming everything will be okay, you're flirting with disaster. Depending on the venue, you may have a lot to do. If it's a big occasion, then you'll need to develop immediate rapport with the organizer. Your relationship with the chairman will have a subtle effect on the tone of voice she uses to introduce you. As for the technician, just remember that only God has more power over your presentation.

Check the layout of the room

- Is the promised equipment there? Immediately check every detail down to felt pens and rubbish bin.

- Are all the visual aids in the best location?

- Is the audience going to be comfortable? Does the air conditioning need turning up or down? Will they be able to see? Will they have sun shining directly on them?

Check that everything works and that you can work everything.

- Make sure you know which buttons to push. The audience will forgive only so much bumbling about trying to figure how things work. Make sure the laptop and the data-projector are talking to each other. Get the image straight and focused.

- Are you dependent on someone else to change the slides? Rehearse your cues and signals.

- If you have sound effects, make sure that they're at the right level. If it's background, the audience must be able to hear your words without being distracted.

- For big venues, check the lighting to be directed at you. Best is two lights, 45° to each side of centre and 45° up from the horizontal. And remember that even if you can't see your audience, they need to see you well lit. Walking in and out of the pool of light will have the same effect as switching your audience on and off.

Give special attention to sound system and lectern

Either of them can seriously affect your authority.

- *Is the lectern too high?* If the highest part is above your sternum, it is, and you'll need to find a box. And don't hesitate to use it. A very short former New Zealand cabinet minister used to carry a box to the lectern, step up onto it and give impressive, authoritative speeches.

- *Check how to speak into the microphone.* Each microphone type has its own personality. Does it rub on your jacket when you move? For lapel mikes, can you turn your head and still be heard?

- *Is the microphone at the right sound level?* Surprise the technician by telling her that in spite of the microphone, you're still planning to raise your voice to project. The microphone needs only enough "level" to make sure you reach into the far corners of the room.

Regardless of microphone, a large audience must see
and hear you making an effort to reach them.

It's an odd, distracting sensation to sit in an audience, hearing words but seeing and hearing the presenter making no effort to reach you. It can also have a curious muffling effect that will make it hard for the audience to hear the words even though there's plenty of sound. (See also *Bigger audiences want you to be bigger* p88)

- *What kind of microphone?* There are three main choices. For most, the first choice is the lapel mike, though the sound is usually not top quality and it's prone to feedback problems.

  Next best is the hand-held radio mike which high quality sound and the comfort of something to hold.

  There's the fixed lectern mike, which works if you really have no intention of getting out from behind the lectern.

  And you do still find hand-held mikes on the end of a long cord. Take care moving around; the danger is that you can become a walking spindle, providing comic relief while you try to talk about the need for more dignity and decorum at staff meetings.

  For more on microphones, see p91.

Check how you're going to be introduced

Beware of inappropriate introductions. You may not want a fanfare of your virtues and accomplishments when you're about to announce the closing of the factory.

The final count-down

Tune into the audience as they arrive

When the first audience member walks in, your presentation is under way. Meet some individually. That's also one of the best ways of overcoming pre-performance nerves, because knowing and recognizing a few individuals transforms an audience into a gathering of real people. When you talk to arriving individuals:

Shake them by the hand. The Romans are credited with inventing the handshake as a way of showing they were not armed. They shook hands all the way up to the elbow, which might look over-enthusiastic if you do it. It's a subtle art: a reasonably firm grip and a shake that lasts no more than three pumps, easy on the grip if it's man-to-woman. Even man-to-man, take care;

you don't want men in your audience nursing crushed fingers and wondering if you're over-compensating for some deficiency.

Remember and use their names. The sweetest of sounds is our own name. Each time someone uses it, we are painted more vividly into our own landscape. We can't help but respond positively to someone who makes the effort to use our name. Here are two methods for remembering.

    Use a rhyming word. A nonsense rhyme works, but it's better if the word has meaning. "Hi, I'm Polly." *Polly. Molly, good golly Miss Molly. Good golly miss Polly!*

    Or use association. "Hi, Trevor. I'm Sue." *Trevor. Hair needs a cut. Hairy head. Hairy head Trevor. Hairy head Trevor.*

Listen to them. I mean fully listen. Eleventh-hour contact like this will alert you to audience mood, feeling or opinion that you have missed. Many individuals will fall all over themselves to let you know their attitude to the forthcoming presentation. Vital stuff. Second, when you develop rapport with an individual, you lay the foundations of a subtle rapport with the entire audience.

Listen to other speakers

How are the other speakers interacting with the audience? What mood is the audience showing them? The answers will make subtle, appropriate differences to your style without you even trying.

    Besides, you can almost always count on a previous speaker to give you something to bounce off. An example: you take the floor, look sadly at the previous speaker and say, "I'm sorry Frank, I think you've got it all wrong with that tree hut. We built ours so that we can move in when the children drive us insane." Rapport, even before you begin the first prepared word. Good debaters always listen to each other, looking for ammunition.

Command yourself with your performance key

Look ahead. The chapter starts on page 65

Rehearse the spotlight, city-view and suburb headings

The first few sentences are usually the hardest to get out confidently. Mentally rehearse the opening ideas, though not every word or you'll sound stiff. If you can, avoid the prompt notes at the beginning. It looks less than convincing to need a piece of paper to tell you when to say "Welcome" or "Thank you" or "Good morning".

It's even less convincing to do the same thing in the middle of a city-view. "Today I'm going to convince you that our strategic plan is a matter of..." (hesitation, looking at paper) "... life and death."

How to overcome persistent symptoms of fear

Obviously, in the long run, it's best to deal to the fear itself—and much of this book is devoted to that. Change your mind, change your feelings. Correct your thinking about fear and the fear itself will loosen its grip.

However, modern neuroscience has also established that when you change your physical response to any stimulus, that affects the wiring of your brain. In other words, deal to the symptoms of fear and you will also be dealing to the fear itself. That may seem a back-to-front approach to handling fear, but it works.

Here are two tips for dealing with the excess symptoms of fear.

When you speak, does your throat feel tight and your voice sound as if it has been squeezed out through a strainer? Do you think everyone can hear the shake in your voice? If so…

try this… Find a quiet spot and hum at a pitch that makes the soft area under your chin vibrate. As you do so, allow the vibrations to spread a feeling of relaxation through your throat and down towards your shoulders.

OR: tilt your head back and push your jaw at the ceiling for a few seconds. You should feel tension in the muscles under your chin. Put a couple of fingers over your bottom teeth and pull slowly but firmly downward, putting pressure on the hinge of the jaw. Smoothly increase and decrease the pressure.

Also, only drink lukewarm liquids. Iced drinks will put your larynx into the Antarctic which is not a region known for producing opera singers. Don't drink carbonated liquids unless you want to belch unintentionally and spectacularly into the microphone.

But perhaps your symptoms are more extensive. Heart racing? Dry mouth? Hands shaking? Constant worry that you'll perform badly? If so, here's the best symptom–taming device I know:

try this... *The vagus nerve squeeze*
Empty your lungs (by pulling in your stomach, not contracting your chest). Breathe in slowly and deeply through your nose (pushing out your stomach, not expanding your chest). Hold for three or four seconds. Exhale very slowly, this time through your mouth. When half the air is gone, partially block the flow of air by pressing your lips close together like a flute player, so that you have to tense your stomach muscles to keep on exhaling. Now, keep forcing the air out until you don't have even a whisper of air left.

Repeat the exercise three times, but also use your imagination. On the inhale, visualize lines of energy flowing from the audience to you. On the exhale, push the lines of energy out through your feet, through the ground and up into the audience. Doctors will tell you that this type of breathing acts on the vagus nerve which acts on the heart, slowing it. Clearly, it also affects the oxygenation of the blood.

That's a very effective way to deal to most symptoms of fear. But maybe even that isn't enough...

For the truly terrified

Are you one who says that the word is not nervousness, but terror? Are your symptoms the same as for terror? Does your body even know the difference? When the spotlight goes on you, do you sweat, do your hands shake and feel clammy, does your heart race? Is your breathing ragged? Does your voice tremble? Do you feel nauseous before you start? For some, it's so bad they throw up the night before and lose all sleep. Some wonder why their body is acting as if it was taking orders from a foreign power. Many who suffer badly have had a traumatic experience at an early age—typically between the ages of six and 14—perhaps being mocked by schoolmates or parents, feeling shame or humiliation.

If that's you, then I admire your courage and willpower in coming this far.

Unfortunately, courage and willpower alone may not be enough. That's because your terror responses have been built in so deeply, for so long, that they now come snarling directly out of your subconscious.

There is a solution.

First, it's important to understand what's really happening. If you are terrified of public speaking, it may well be that early in your life, your mind made this link: public speaking means humiliation. And that link was made often enough and passionately enough to affect your subconscious. That, of course, is bad enough. But in extreme cases it goes further. Fear of experiencing that humiliation again deepens the effect on the subconscious. It's a vicious cycle. Now the link is: public speaking means terror. Little wonder that your subconscious is hard of hearing when your conscious mind says, *This is ridiculous, I'm only talking to a few people I know. It shouldn't affect me like this.* Your body still reacts as if a white pointer is circling you in the water.

The solution is to break that link and re-programme your subconscious. To do that, we'll borrow from a discipline known as neuro-linguistic programming, changing the association from public speaking means terror, to public speaking means pleasure.

You may think that sounds unrealistic. But your subconscious has no concept of reality, truth or untruth. It just goes on obeying your orders and shaping your life. Oh yes, you're giving it orders all the time, usually without knowing it; there's a whole life-transforming significance to this, but for now we'll stick to public speaking. Follow me through Kiri's story. (I've changed her name.)

At the age of nine, Kiri made a mistake in her words when she was talking in front of the school assembly. The sight of pointing fingers and the sound of mocking laughter sank in deeply as searing humiliation. When I met her, she was an adult, recently promoted to senior management, and desperately trying to overcome extreme symptoms of fear of public speaking. When she was not performing, she could speak to the rest of the training group without too much problem. But the moment it was her turn to come out the front, her body would start to shake, her mouth would dry up, her hands would go clammy and various other symptoms would torture her body. She was also furious with herself that she couldn't control those symptoms—a judgement that only exaggerated her problems.

I asked her to do some homework that night that would provide her with a special physical movement—a trigger that would change the association of public speaking with fear, and would stop her body going into the too-familiar downward spiral. As you read through the first three steps, notice that there is no mention of public speaking.

1. Think of something in your past which has given you immense pleasure. If it's the single greatest pleasure you've ever had, so much the better. Feelings of love, exhilaration, triumph, compassion and pride are all excellent tools for programming your subconscious. Luxuriate in that pleasure again. Feel the effects on your body.

2. Decide on a simple physical movement to use as a programming trigger. It should be inconspicuous, such as touching the knuckle of your index finger, or pressing forefinger into thumb.
3. Spend significant time, as vividly and emotionally as possible, alternating between imagining 1. and doing 2.

    Suppose, for example, that your pleasure source is the way you felt when you crossed the finish line and won the swimming contest. Imagine. You stand up, gasping for air, water clears from your goggles, and you realize that you've done it. You've won. Everyone is looking at you and cheering and applauding. You feel exhilaration and triumph. Touch forefinger to thumb. You've won! Exhilaration! Triumph! Touch forefinger to thumb. Yes! What exhilaration! Your whole body is feeling it again. Touch forefinger to thumb. And so on. It's not the imagining itself, but the feeling that makes this work. The more passionate and carried away you are, the better. Lose yourself in it. Associate that tiny physical movement again and again and again with pleasure.

That night, Kiri carried out those first three steps. When she woke in the morning, she repeated step three, and she continued it before and after breakfast and in the car on the way to the training.

4. As you go out in front of the audience, press your programming trigger. Press it again just as you begin to speak.

Then it was Kiri's turn. As she rose from her seat and came forward she pressed thumb to forefinger; and again as she opened her mouth to speak. And something wonderful happened—most of her symptoms of fear melted away. Then, when she realized the significance of what she had achieved, even those last echoes of fear vanished. The other trainees were open-mouthed and gave her huge applause when she finished.

By the end of that day, Kiri was thoroughly enjoying herself. It was obvious to everyone that she had become the most confident speaker in the room. When she left, she was walking on air.

What could that device do for you?

PRESENTATION NOTES

On a blank sheet, create a city-view, brainstorm, link ideas, then transfer information onto this form.

Audience ....

Date ....

Opening spotlight

City-view

Suburbs

Streets

Closing spotlight

"It's not what you tell them that counts. It's what they remember."

How do I make my audio-visual aids effective?

OR How to use audio-visual aids without inflicting death by PowerPoint

> "I urge you to incorporate all the visual aids you can to support, but not make, your main arguments." *Tom Hopkins, How to Master the Art of Selling.*

Caution

Recently I spoke with a woman who was the 13th speaker on a Friday afternoon at a major symposium; something of a challenge, I'm sure you'll agree. When her session was over, a small group came to her and said, "We loved your speech..." Her head was about to swell with pride when they added something: "...because you didn't use *PowerPoint.*"

Data-shows are the most potentially useful, yet abysmally misused development in the history of audio-visual aids. When PowerPoint arrived, many presenters thought, *Now I too can look great.* It offered them wizardry, enabling them to use whizz-bang effects until audience eyeballs rolled in their sockets. Sorry, but if your un-stated message is *please admire my great audio-visual effects,* then your stated message is likely to be overwhelmed. Your audiences will leave, thinking, *What was that about?* and sympathising with the angry Pentagon official who issued orders to all armed services data-show users: "Keep it simple. Get to the point."

Each electronic effect is like finding a word written in caps in a letter. Would you write a letter with every second word in caps? I don't think so, unless you've been skipping your medication. It's visual shouting.

Each visual effect is like a shout.
Constant shouting causes audiences to tune you out.

Visual aids must enhance, not overwhelm, your message.

How to prepare

Choosing content

Make a radical ground-breaking decision. Start a trend which will wake increasingly comatose audiences and once again have them applauding presenters.

> Effective presenters are supported by their data-show
> —not the other way around.

That decision alone will transform your choice of content and your impact on the audience. It means, for example, that you'll refuse to be stuck to the screen, unable to give the audience a break, showing slide after slide after slide, each another nail in the coffin of your presentation. In particular, it means that you won't any longer sit down and type out your entire word presentation on the screen.

> On screen,
> words are weak, pictures are powerful.

All right, I'll admit that there are two good reasons for putting text on the screen. First: when everyone must see an exact wording. Second: when a list of words must be seen as a whole.

If you must use text, write in headlines

Often I ask those who come to my workshops, What's the single most annoying thing presenters do with PowerPoint? The answer is almost unanimous. "I hate it when the presenter puts up full sentences, then reads out what I can see for myself." They add, "It's insulting. It's boring. I go to sleep."

There's an easy fix:

> Write in headlines
> and add value with your commentary

An example: write on the screen: **Reset top tray first** and plan to add value by explaining why. (See also *Avoiding 'this is a cow'* p62).

However, we can't make a blanket rule of not reading out words on the screen. A quote, for example, often works better if you do read it out, as long as your tone and emphasis give it a meaning the audience would not get from just reading.

Make each slide relevant to each audience

I know; it's a big ask if you have different kinds of audience for the same topic. But, suppose you show technicians detailed specs for the new telephone equipment. Then how much do you achieve if you show the same slide to telephone receptionists?

Keep each slide simple

Simple and uncluttered. Make sure it contains only the information related to your message. For graphs, you'll see a good example back on page six. That format would be suitable for a data-show because it contains only the bare minimum needed to convey the message. Resist every temptation to throw up a comprehensive table of figures just to make a point about one cell. You'll end up saying to the audience, "Look at this number down here; yes here it is: 13th row, 8th column."

Keeping it simple usually means more work. For the more scientific presenters, it may be best to have a simplified version on the screen (to illustrate the main point) and the more comprehensive version on the handout.

But do add (relevant) visual interest

Figures on a graphic are often so dry they have little impact on the audience. For example, divorces in 1976: 684. Increase in a year: 9.5%. Got the emotional impact? Of course not. So in your graphic you may need to add relevant visual interest, preferably relevant human interest.

- *Add a picture.* It could be a drawing of an object, a cartoon, even a photograph. If the picture can highlight an emotion, so much the better. An example: for divorce statistics—a picture of a couple back to back, the space between them for your numbers.

- *Make your graphs out of pictures.* An example: a graph of the rise in spending on armaments may only register as a sloping line to your audience. But what if that line were the barrel of a Scorpion tank?

Another example: you run a retail flower company and you want a chart that compares sales of your different varieties of flowers. Imagine, on the screen, a single flower for each variety, each sized to represent it's sales figures, each with a percentage number above it.

Make numbers fit the audience

So you want to be accurate? Fine. Every digit in the figure 4.96% should be there for bankers discussing interest rates. But would you really show a figure of that accuracy to parents concerned with injury accidents at school? It has no meaning for them. It's better shown on the screen as 1 in 20, or 5%. You can qualify verbally, by saying, "Almost one in twenty".

Make printing large

Here's a rough guideline for a data-show. Use a sans serif font (easier to read on the screen) with a minimum font size of 18. However it's often so important to get a whole diagram onto one slide you may need to go smaller.

Never fly in your words

Our surveys show that at least two thirds of most audiences hate it. Left or right, up or down, audiences have been exposed to hyperactive words too often. Mentally, they beg, *Please, just show us the list.* You might object that if you simply show the whole list, how is the audience going to know which point you're discussing?" No problem; you could easily animate a simple marker (such as a fat dot or a tick) to move down the list. You could use a pointer or a hand. Or you could just tell them. ("Second point", "third" etc).

But here's another solution, which also answers another audience need.

Pre-exposure of lists: show the whole, highlight the part

If there was a top ten of audience irritants, it would have to include presenters who start with a blank space then reveal lists point by point.

> Audiences must glimpse the whole
> before they can fully relate to the part.

It's called pre-exposure: revealing the whole before discussing the part. You might remember this from chapter two: tell them what you're going to tell them, then tell them. Pre-exposure.

Software data-show programmes usually allow you to pre-expose lists without overdoing the special effects. First, show the list at reduced contrast. (For example light blue words on a dark blue background, with enough contrast to make it readable.) Then, with each click of the advance button, the next item on the list changes colour (say light blue to bright yellow) and the audience never loses sight of the whole list.

In this black and white illustration, bold lettering represents a change of colour.

First frame	Animate 1	Animate 2	Animate 3
HANDLING ANGER	HANDLING ANGER	HANDLING ANGER	HANDLING ANGER
Feelings	**Feelings**	Feelings	Feelings
Facts	Facts	**Facts**	Facts
Follow-through	Follow-through	Follow-through	**Follow-through**

How to deliver visual aids to an audience

For some, it's a surprise that there might be rules of performance just for visual aids. Don't you just show the stuff and talk? Unfortunately that's exactly what most presenters do, not only neglecting a wonderful source of impact, but actually killing off audience interest.

Introduce your presentation with nothing on the screen

In our training sessions we show audiences two ways of starting a presentation and ask them to choose which they prefer. Either a presenter introducing the session with the title slide up, or the presenter introducing the session with nothing on the screen at all. The result is very clear—almost 100 per cent choose the second. They want to get to grips with the presenter's presence first.

By all means have a title slide, but show it as people come into the room, then lose it before your first words.

The core visual-aids principle (does not apply to data-shows)

If you went down the street speaking to cars, mailboxes and fence posts, you would soon be talking to either a policeman or some sincere men in white coats. So, when we're in front of an audience and need good human contact, why do we talk to whiteboards, flip chart paper, and own speech notes? Many talk to their speech notes even when they're not reading anything.

Here's my favourite definition of the core principle of visual aids:

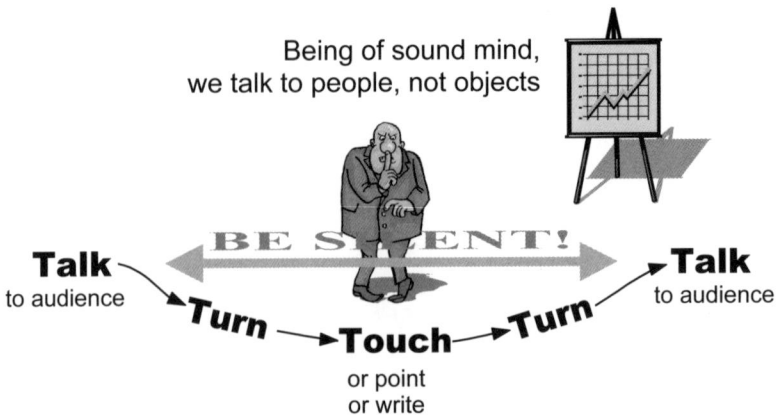

1. Talk only while your eyes are engaged to the eyes of the audience. Start turning your body to the whiteboard while your head and eyes stay on the audience for the last words. Don't send the last words to the wall or window on the way around.

2. Stay silent while you touch or point or write.

3. Turn your head and eyes quickly back to the audience. Start talking only when your eyes have re-engaged with audience eyes (not just looking in their direction). Let your body catch up to your head in its own time.

With this method you demonstrate that your desire is not to get out the facts, but to engage the facts to your audience. Of course it does mean that you have to become comfortable with silence. Which is exactly what effective presenters do; and the best use the silence deliberately. But if you're not convinced…

try this… Imagine sitting in the audience watching yourself as the presenter. Imagine that this replica of yourself drops his eyes away from yours and keeps right on talking to his notes. Every now and then he looks up at everyone, but soon returns to the comfort of the notes.

But now change the picture. Imagine that when your second self needs to look at the paper, he stops talking before he cuts eye contact, and with complete confidence he gets his information, looks up again and doesn't speak until he has eye contact with someone.

Which replica of yourself did you like best? The first or the second? If the answer is the first, apply for early retirement. Even without any visual-aids, we tune out presenters who smother us with wall-to-wall words.

The exception to the visual-aids principle (applies to all data-shows)

The exception applies to anything projected onto a large screen. This time you will be talking to an object and you'll be also be moving part of your body that most people will not see.

Few presenters know this subtle piece of magic. It's magic, because it can instantly change the audience from merely enduring your data-show, to wanting to be there. Subtle, because you can create that magic effect with something so simple and so inconspicuous the audience won't know how you did it. (So subtle, it took our company several training sessions to work out what was really going on.).

First, the psychology.

> Your audience has a subconscious yet strong desire for you to look at their screen *with them*.

That does not mean you should decamp to the back of the room. Far from it.

Think of how data-show presenters normally stand. They're out the front, slightly to one side of the screen, facing us directly while the screen is busy. Consider this. Their body language says, *Look at me*. But the screen is also, in its own way, saying, *Look at me*. That's visual ambiguity and, without knowing it consciously, the audience feels uncertainty. The cost? Loss of impact of your screen message. Loss of attention. Glazed eyes. Death by PowerPoint.

The cure?

It's as simple as pointing your feet in a different direction.

What? Even behind a lectern? Where no one can see your feet?

Yes, even there; because turning your feet puts a small but very important twist into your entire body. A vital signal to the audience. So, when your first slide hits the screen…

60 How do I make my audio-visual aids effective?

1. Look at the screen and point your feet halfway between the screen and the centre of the audience.

2. Stay silent, looking at the screen with audience. Give them just enough time to take in the slide as a whole (as if it were a photograph), but not enough to read detail.

3. Turn to audience to begin talking.

4. Talk to both audience and screen, moving upper body only.

Point your feet half way between the screen and the centre of the audience. It removes visual ambiguity, making the rest of your body signal to the audience, *look at the screen, not me.* It also signals, *I am looking at the screen with you.*

Talk to the screen?

Yes. This is the exception to the don't-talk-to-objects rule. In fact you must talk to the screen; because you have just told the audience (with your body) *Look at the screen and I will look with you.* But of course you're still the presenter; so now you talk back and forth, with your feet still pointed halfway between screen and audience. Do you see the beauty of this? You have removed the visual ambiguity from the situation. Effectively you have said, *You can look at me if you like, but the dominant visual message is on the screen.* Your audience will be pleasantly surprised that they were not bored and they won't know how you did it.

So simple.

But you may not believe it until you try it out. Get a few colleagues together and experiment with it. Understanding that the audience wants you to join them looking at the screen will quickly lead you to refinements:

- Pre-announce each slide. For example, say, "Now, let's have a look at the schematics." Click for next slide, look at screen, point feet (1.), stay looking with audience in silence (2.), turn to audience and speak

(3.). Pre-announcing helps the audience focus on what's coming. To achieve it, you have to know (or have notes on) what's slide comes next.

- In step 2, while you're looking in silence with the audience at the new material, quickly glance back at the audience. That glance—perhaps no more than half a second—says I'm checking that you can see okay and that you're taking this in.

- If, in your enthusiasm, you stride up close to the screen to point at something (a good thing to do for variety), you can no longer talk to the screen. It's back to visual-aid basics. Point silently, turn silently, talk. It looks good, it looks emphatic.

Don't use the screen as a prompt

More bad news for most presenters. Audiences are irritated when you prompt yourself from the screen. Screen-prompting tells them you don't know your stuff. Conversely they are not irritated if you have a simple list on hand to keep you ahead of the screen.

Don't engage with your own computer screen

Don't talk to your computer screen while the audience looks at the big screen. The body language message is *You are in one place, I am in another.* The audience has to work very hard to take in your message. Some, inevitably, will feel disconnected and switch off.

Don't become a prisoner of your own data-show

Most presenters feel trapped as soon as they start the first slide. They feel threatened by interruptions and they definitely don't want the order of the slides changed. So two disturbing things happen:

Split attention. The presenter stays with that picture of the new library when the topic turns to Mongolian horse flu, so the audience doesn't know what to focus on. The solution is simple:

- When the topic changes, blank the screen. In PowerPoint, just push the letter B on your computer (the screen will go blank), point your feet back at the audience (reclaiming their visual attention) then talk as normal. Then, when you're ready to return to the screen, push B again and the original picture will re-appear.

That keeps you in charge, not the data-show. You use the screen for as long as it enhances your message and not a second more.

Slide grind. We've all seen it. We're on slide 23 and someone asks to see that 2nd slide again. So the presenter grinds us back through every slide, including all the animations. It's a visual assault deserving of a prison term. Here's the solution:

- Keep a list of slide topics and numbers. Then, if you want to go back to slide 2, press 2 then enter. Want to return to slide 23? Press 23 and enter. It doesn't get simpler than that.

Avoiding 'this is a cow'

Television news chief reporters will often use the phrase to criticise a rookie reporter's item. It says that the reporter is telling people what they can see perfectly well for themselves, implying that they are stupid.

Show the picture, then add value with your commentary.

Some examples:

Picture

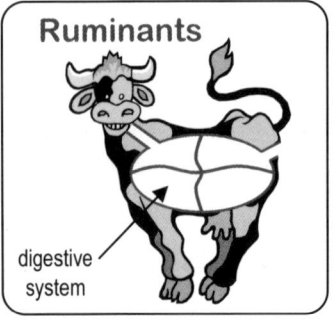

Commentary

"Here's a cow and this is a diagram showing the ruminant digestive system with four chambers."

 This doesn't work. We can see for ourselves almost everything being said. It's insulting.

How do I make my audio-visual aids effective? 63

Picture

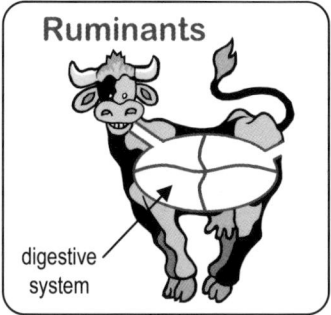

Commentary
(after a pause)
"If Daisy didn't have more than one stomach, she wouldn't be able to digest grass. The chamber on the top left is…"

 This works well. The commentary adds value to the picture, saying nothing we can't see for ourselves.

Or, you may want to make words the dominant feature, supported by pictures.

Picture

> **Ruminants**
> - Ruminants are cud-chewing, cloven hoofed animals.
> - The ruminant digestive system involves four stomach chambers.

Commentary
(after a pause)
"The first point… Other ruminants? Sheep, goats, deer, and giraffes."

(after another pause)
"Second point… two of those chambers are for fermenting or pre-digestion… that's what leads to the cud-chewing…"

 This only just works. There are full sentences on the screen but the commentary avoids repeating the same words and adds material we can't see for ourselves.

64   How do I make my audio-visual aids effective?

Picture

Ruminants
- Cud-chewing, cloven hoofed.
- Four stomach chambers.

Commentary

(after a pause)
"First point... Not just the cow, but also sheep, goats, deer, giraffes."

(after a pause)
"Second point... Two chambers are for pre-digestion fermenting, then up to the mouth for more chewing, then back to the next two chambers for the finishing touches."

 This works. It's written in headlines and the commentary adds only what we can't see for ourselves.

Be silent with every visual change

I've made the point already, but note that it also applies to animations within each slide. Eighty per cent of us are more influenced by the visual sense than any other; so much so, that our other senses shut down briefly when visual changes happen. Even a subtle change to a single screened word—say a brightening of colour—needs a moment of silence while you look at it anew and the audience looks at it with you and takes it in.

There might only be a second in it, but that second is part of the rhythm of the dance that calls for three partners: you, the visual aids, and the audience.

 # How do I work out my personal performance key?

The self-command that liberates excellent performance—automatically

Have you ever given a presentation while trying to remember a list of instructions on how to perform? Maintain eye contact, don't talk to the paper, move around, don't click the pen, put in pauses, don't 'um', remember to pause, etc. Such bullet-point lists can be lengthy, they don't work very well, and can often increase anxiety.

But what if you had just one phrase—a personal performance key—that would liberate all the right stuff, automatically, when you need it?

- In this chapter, you'll select (or work out) your own trial personal performance key.

- In the near future, you'll refine or change your performance key.

- In the years ahead, your key will become a natural part of you and you won't even have to think about it.

The target here is a state of mind and body psychologists call 'flow'. When you're in flow you perform effortlessly; words come easily, time flies, you feel exhilarated and in perfect control. When you're in flow, your conscious mind does not think about the components of good speaking.

Sports people call flow 'the zone'. Recently, sports scientists in the UK studied professional cricketers. They used stop frame pictures to work out the batsman's anticipation time—that is, when does the batsman start to move his body according to where he thinks the ball is heading?[5] The result was around one tenth of a second *before the ball left the bowler's hand.* Think about that. You might call it uncanny, you might call it instinct; but clearly, the conscious mind, alone, isn't enough to explain it. Imagine the batsman consciously trying to analyze dozens of physical indicators from the bowler before deciding how to move. Impossible. For top performance, the subconscious is in the driving seat long before the conscious mind resumes control.

Top presenters trust and train their subconscious. Releasing flow from the subconscious, at will, may be the single most rewarding skill you can get from this book. The irony is that to release flow from the subconscious you'll use your conscious mind.

How?

Certainly not with bullet points; don't try to remember lists in this chapter. Instead, look for a single idea that pushes your on-button. We'll call it your personal performance key—a phrase you'll use as an attitude adjuster and self-command just before you begin speaking.

I'm going to outline five popular performance keys that have emerged from my training workshops. They won't all suit you—everyone responds in different ways—but the chances are that one will. Look especially for a concept that rouses your feelings, then alter the wording to suit you. For example: one of the keys in the following pages is *Let go of the bush.* As you'll see, it refers to releasing fears. One trainee, a firm Christian, changed the wording to *Get out of the boat,* a reminder of Jesus telling Peter to release his fear, hop overboard and take a stroll. For her passions, it was perfect.

In this chapter more than any other, deliberately give your intellect second place to your feelings—or instinct. Peter Ustinov said it, albeit tongue in cheek, "The duty of intelligence is merely to correct the instinct in cases of emergency." The world's top performers would understand exactly what he's talking about.

---

[5] *The Human Mind*, Robert Winston, 2004

Here's one popular performance key you might choose for unlocking flow.

 **1** GET ENGAGED TO THE AUDIENCE!
Alternatives: Get over yourself and be with the audience! It's about the audience. It's not about you!

Look especially at that last alternative. This is definitely in the category of strange but true. It really is not about you, unless you make it so. It's supposed to be about the marriage between your message and the audience. For many, that thought alone is an instant performance key in its own right.

One of the reasons *Get engaged* works so well for so many is that it confronts them with something they've done to themselves without ever knowing it. They've allowed fear to intensify the spotlight on themselves to such a degree that they no longer see the audience as real people. They can't be with the audience, they can only talk in front of them. The long-suffering audience is cut off, like aliens here on Earth to witness acute suffering.

Who is the most important person in the world? No, it's not you. It's the person you're with right now. This Buddhist thinking has a lot to offer presenters and leaders. When you are fully present for the individuals in the audience, the audience will be drawn to you and respect you.

Can you see what a self-creating trap it is to focus so much on your worries? If you water only the weeds in your garden, guess what grows fastest. If you allow light to reach only the weeds, fertilise only the weeds, attend only to the weeds, guess what flourishes in your garden.

Look back at the grim reaper figure in the cartoon (p65). When you're asked to speak, how often does your grim reaper keep up a worried monologue like this: *I'm no good at this. I'll say the wrong thing. I'll forget my words. I speak in a monotone. I'll be boring. My ears stick out. My bald spot is obvious. I'll have no authority because I'm too fat / skinny / lumpy / young/ old / wrinkled / saggy / naff / pigeon-toed /………… (choose your own).*

The real problem is not the supposed truth of such worries. The problem is the worries. Got the difference? Worried thoughts create what you worry about, thus appearing to prove the worries true. It is the thought, *I have no authority* that lowers your authority, not any supposed reality. Your personal authority is no more nor less than what you deeply believe it to be and your belief is built on ten thousand thoughts. All of life is like this. It's the law of attraction: What you think, you become; what you feel, will follow; what you focus on, you get.

Also, evict any thought that your physical body has a bearing on your personal authority. It simply isn't the point—nobody cares unless you make them care by worrying about it. Effective presenters who will never model underwear do get thunderous applause and standing ovations.

So, how do I get rid of my worries?

Directly? Don't even try—that's much too hard. Instead, shift your focus.

Shift your focus from your worries
to the needs, desires and concerns of the audience.

That's how to deal to your worries. Starve them of attention.

But the audience is exactly what I'm afraid of!

No, it's you you're really afraid of, which means you're still focused on your self. Instead, focus on the audience needs, desires and concerns.

They have needs? You mean there are real people out there?

Take a look—out beyond that spotlight you have trained so glaringly on yourself. See? Not aliens but real human beings. They live, they breathe, they have thoughts and feelings.

Good grief. You mean this isn't about me?

try this... Look again at the grim reaper character. Imagine that this part of you is a character sitting on your shoulder. Now turn to that character and say to it quietly, *How dare you put yourself ahead of these people waiting to hear me speak.* Rough, isn't it? If you stay self-conscious you're telling the audience that your needs are more important than theirs. Which insults the audience. No matter how kind and understanding they are, if you rate them low in importance they can't help but do the same to you.

Want to reverse that? Of course you do. Then engage with the audience by putting them first. Ironic, isn't it? You serve your own needs best by forgetting your needs and looking after the audience.

"There was a man, though some did count him mad.
The more he cast away the more he had." *W.S. Plummer*

try this... *Practise smiling with your eyes only.*
Look in the mirror. Try allowing warmth to show in your eyes without smiling with your mouth—you can relax the

muscles around your mouth but you mustn't smile. Imagine you're in front of your best friend. You'll find it affects particular muscles round your eyes and temples. Let it.

Do you like the people in your audience? Allow that liking to show. Do you like your message? Do you believe in it? Is it worth convincing your audience? Allow your answer to generate your natural warmth.

Your own wording?

If *Get engaged to the audience* looks like a good key for you, how could you re-word it to suit you? What phrase or sentence, used as a self-command, will liberate all the right stuff? Here are a few examples others have chosen:

    Get over yourself!   It's about them!
    Be *with* them!   Talk to real people!

Just one caution. Don't use the word 'don't' in a performance key—you'll end up nourishing a negative. If you don't believe me, try this: don't imagine a pink elephant.

2   LET GO OF THE BUSH!
Alternatives: Release your fears and fly! Let go! Let it go!

Did you hear the one about the man who had a couple too many at the local tavern?

Well, on the way home, the man finds himself lost. He negotiates his way into every obstacle in his path, using the Lord's name as his compass, until he finally falls over an almighty big cliff. But, a little way down the cliff face, he just manages to grasp hold of a bush.

So there he is, hanging, with the sea churning on the rocks far below. And he calls out towards the top of the cliff, "Help! Help! Is there anyone there?"

"God here," a voice booms down to

him from above. "Just let go of the bush, believe, and you will be saved."

He considers this. He looks up at the bush, he looks down at the sea and the rocks, and he looks straight out ahead. Then he calls up to the top of the cliff, "Is there anyone else up there?"

It's the letting go that's relevant here. This is no intellectual concept—it's an attitude, a feeling. Let the bush represent the bundle of doubts and anxieties that make us grasp false securities, like speaking in monotones and officialese, and talking to paper rather than people.

You know those anxieties, don't you? There were some in the last performance key. Here are some more: *Am I going to forget the words...? Did I remember to brush my hair...? I hope I don't drop my notes... I'm standing awkwardly... I can't seem to focus on anyone.... etc... etc... etc...* To allow a litany like that into your head when you're trying to make a presentation is like allowing a herd of elephants to weed the lettuces. And yet you can't fight such destructive self-talk point by point. It's much easier to work directly on the attitude behind them and re-programme your subconscious.

Tell yourself in internally reverberating tones: *let go of the bush!*

It's an act of faith in yourself. The biggest risk in life is to take no risk, and the time to take a risk is now. It's like thinking, *Well, if I hang here I'm dead anyway. I've got nothing to lose. Time to release my fears and allow myself to fly.*

Have you noticed similarities with the first performance key? The performance keys open doors, which all lead into the same garden: that marvellous inner strength which waits patiently in all of us.

try this... It's an imagination exercise. Place yourself in front of an audience. As you speak, deliberately think up all the doubts you have. Exaggerate the picture and get as much detail as you can. Deliberately conjure up awkward body language, word-stumbling, stuttering, apologizing constantly for yourself. Watch how it's not your inability but your fear that generates all the mistakes. Watch the awful pity on the faces of the audience as they see you suffering.

Now. Laugh. Say to yourself, *This mental rubbish is getting in my way. Why am I hanging on to it? I'll let it go, all at once.* Imagine it forming into the shape of a bush over your head, then open up your hands and let it go.

Finally, replace that dismal first picture. This time, see yourself relaxed and enjoying the occasion. You're speaking warmly, you're interacting comfortably with individuals, taking a real interest in how your topic is going down with them. You're enjoying yourself. If you enjoy yourself, so will the audience. So obvious, so effective.

Does that push your buttons or does it leave you unmoved? Somewhere in between? Compare with other performance keys to come.

Your own wording?

If *Let go of the bush* looks like a good key for you, how could you re-word it to make it exactly right? Examples others have chosen:

        Let go!   Walk on water!
        Fly!   Drop Linus's blanket!

Notice that last phrase? Drop Linus's blanket. (In case you haven't met the idea, it refers to a cartoon child, Linus, who is only ever seen with his comfort blanket.) A wise young woman chose that phrase. She recognized that she had been taking refuge in the comfortable familiarity of her own worries about speaking. Which is so true of life. Many people do not want to abandon the distressing circumstances they know; the risk of letting go is too great.

3   PASS THE PASSION TEST!

Alternatives: *Show* you're keen to explain! *Show* that you want the audience to get the message!

"Nothing great was ever achieved without enthusiasm."
Ralph Waldo Emerson.

"There can be no transforming of darkness into light and of apathy into movement without emotion." *Carl Jung*

I know. It's a risk. *If I make an effort to display passion, I'll look like a performing clown. People will come up afterwards and offer me tranquillizers.* We each draw a safety line in the mental sand and tell ourselves that if we allow passion to push us over that line, we'll look foolish. Our internal grim reaper murmurs in our heads, *Better to be boring than take the risk of looking foolish.* But do you know where that line really is? For almost all of us, it's not in the look-foolish place at all—it's in the place of take-no-risks at all. In the safety of a training workshop, many people do take the risk and discover to their astonishment that the real look-foolish line in the sand is much further away than they thought. In the last ten years, I could count on the fingers of one hand the number of people who actually overdid the passion.

The trainees who get the most out of the passion test performance key are those most surprised when I stop the camera and ask them this question.

"Tell me, are you interested in this topic?"

"Of course!" they reply, indignant. Is it not obvious? Am I deaf and blind? Am I suffering from an attention deficit condition?

"I don't know that. You're not showing it."

"But..." The speaker looks for support to his colleagues, only to find heads shaking at them. Grinning, but shaking. Uh...uh. You don't look interested to us.

Many, then, adopt this alternative wording for their personal performance key: *show* that you're keen to explain!

A Chinese scientist came to one of the presentation skills workshops. For half a day, she struggled, partly because English was difficult for her, but mostly because she was self-conscious about her heavy accent. She was constantly on the back foot. Then she hit on a subject in which she finally dared to show that she was keen to explain. She role-played giving a welcoming speech to a group of visitors to her house, and it was very important in her tradition that visitors feel welcome. She allowed her enthusiasm to overwhelm all vestiges of self-consciousness, rather like the sun breaking through departing rain clouds. She was so warm, so open-hearted, that when she finished there was a stunned silence, then considerable applause. Whereupon she blushed from head to toe, generating warm laughter.

Yes, she made plenty of mistakes with her pronunciation and grammar, yes, we missed some of her heavily accented words, but we caught every nuance of the heart of her speech and we no longer cared a jot about the mistakes.

When you pass the passion test,
people forgive your mistakes or don't notice them.

Flow makes flaws opaque.

A software salesman from India began the training hunched over, with minimal body language, reluctant eye contact and subdued voice. He told us,

How do I work out my personal performance key? 73

in barely audible words, "People see I speak wrong words and very bad grammar." Later, much to everyone's delight, he suddenly transformed, becoming a pleasure to hear and see. He was in flow.

"How did you do it?" I asked, when the applause stopped. "What made the difference?"

"Now I am understanding," he explained, waving his arms exuberantly. "When I am having passion, no one care about speak wrong words and very bad grammar!"

Exactly.

Passion burns off excess nervous energy.

David Bellamy, who became known as the TV botany man, hardly ever brushed his hair, he flung his arms about as if he was trying to take off, and now and then we could see spittle flying from his mouth. Yet the millions who saw him did not criticize any of those things. And tens of thousands of young people said to themselves, "Wow! Botany is interesting!"

try this...
Silent passion.
Call in a trusted friend for feedback, then practise speaking in half-minute chunks, in silence. That is, you're doing everything—body movements, face and eye movements, jaw and mouth working the words—except that no sound emerges from your mouth. Here's the challenge: your friend has to be able to tell from visual signals alone that you're keen for her to get the message. The important word is 'keen'. You may need to try it a few times, working your body more and more emphatically, before you pass that test. Then, quickly, do it again, this time allowing the words to come out. Expect some applause.

Along the way, did anything happen to your nervousness?

try this...
Read a story passionately to a child. Deliberately act the part of a story teller and imagine a pre-teen child, at least ten years old. Read just two sentences, then—using the same intonations—switch immediately to a serious work-related topic. You might not believe this at first, so you'll need feedback from a friend to help you make this remarkable discovery: the sound of a children's story (early teens) enthusiastically told is almost the same as the sound of an adult presentation well delivered.

Sounds absurd, doesn't it? Talking to a serious adult audience with the intonations of a children's story? Don't dismiss it until you've tried it. The only real difference between the two is our own inhibitions. When we read a story, we're relaxed and our children get our full uninhibited range—voice charged with interest, pitch highs and lows, emphasis, intensity and dramatic silence. When we talk to an adult audience we're often cautious and clamp down on those components, the very components which make us sound interesting.

Recently a trainee using the children's story concept made such a transformation to her business presentations that she re-worded the passion test performance key as 'The Three Bears'. Now the three bears are right there with her when she gives a presentation.

Your own wording?

Could you use the concept *Pass the passion test*? Would any of the alternative wordings above suit you? Some wordings others have chosen:

Be keen to explain!	Show your enthusiasm!
Act passionate!	The three bears!
Act the part!	Speak with your heart!

 **4**   ACT AS IF...!
Alternatives: Fake it until you make it! Act the part until the act becomes the reality!

One day, when I was working as a television journalist, I was sent out to a graveyard—with camera, camera operator and sound operator.

For at least two years, I had been working with a problem. I'd been hired to put a news story together with appropriate pictures and sound. That I could do. I had also been hired to talk to the camera now and then as part of the news item. That I could not do. Every time in that two years, my to-camera clips came up on screen looking awkward and self-conscious. I still don't know why they didn't either train me or fire me.

On this particular day, there was heavy mist in the graveyard. An excellent, moody shot. I had to walk amongst the tomb stones and talk to the camera. On the first take, no surprises; I was uncomfortable and it showed.

"I need to do that again," I said to the camera crew.

They looked at their watches and rolled their eyeballs. I went back and did it again. Take two, which was, if anything, even worse than the first take. I felt terrible. I told them that I would need another take and they did the watches and eyeball trick again with even more exaggeration. In those days, camera crews could be difficult to work with.

But as I walked back to start take three, I had a thought that would turn out to be one of the best discoveries in my life. I knew I was no good at this speaking-to-camera game, and here's the thought: *Why don't I act as if I'm Rodney Bryant.* Rodney was a television presenter with a relaxed, assured on-screen presence.

My third take was so much better than anything I had ever done for television that the camera and sound operators were astonished. Their jaws dropped. Finally one of them said, "Well, why didn't you do that the first time?"

Do you see the beauty of what happened? Yes, it was an act. No, I was not being me. And here's the point: I released myself from the me I believed I was. From that moment I improved dramatically.

'Act as if...' is most popular with people who suffer badly from nervous symptoms. They're the ones who have said too emphatically for too many years, *I am not a public speaker* and programmed their subconscious with that belief.

But what, exactly, is the act?

If you choose this performance key, you have to know the answer to that question. And there are two ways to go about it.

try this... Picture an imaginary ideal presenter. Take time to make this image sharp. Strongly picture what that presenter does. How does she move her head, her arms, her legs? Does she walk with a stride, or a measured pace? How does she stand? Is it with weight on one leg or evenly balanced? How does she look at people? How does she answer a question? How does she use her voice? How emphatic is she on important points? How intense? Does she look as if she wants to be there? What does she do when she makes a mistake? What does that confidence and authority look like? How would it look on you? How does she feel about speaking in public? Could you feel that way?

Clearly this list could go on. And it should; the more time you spend, the more vividly you will paint your ideal presenter into your head. The more vivid the painting, the easier your act will be.

Now, don't just imagine this ideal presenter. Start acting it out—perhaps at home—walking around speaking aloud using your topic material. Get comments from someone you trust. How does this look? How does this sound? Between the laughter and the serious moments, you'll make gains.

How do I work out my personal performance key?

Soon enough, your trusted partner will say to you, 'Hey, that was good. You're really good.' By all means reply that it's really just an act, but you'll know that underneath, the real you is starting to expand.

try this... This time, think of a real person you admire as a speaker. It doesn't have to be someone famous—perhaps a work colleague, a friend or relative. Now do exactly what was in the previous exercise.

You might wonder if there's a danger in this: that if you model yourself on someone known in your company, then people will think you're aping them. Maybe so if you're a born mimic, but in practice it's never a problem. By the time your image of that person is filtered right back through your body and mind, you'll have created a persona that doesn't look anything like the original model. Only you will know. Of course it could come unstuck if you copy an individual idiosyncrasy, such as wringing hands, or sniffing, or slapping the whiteboard to make a point. But if you're serious about this game, you won't be doing that anyway.

In the workshops, in front of a camera, the results of 'Acting as if...' are fascinating. Even the first attempt at acting is often significantly better than any reality that's gone before. But there's often an exchange like this.

"What do you think?" I ask the trainee when the applause dies away.

"It was too much. Way over the top. I was a show pony."

His or her own colleagues promptly and vehemently deny it. "But it wasn't. It was good. Never seen you do it so well." Then I replay the videotape so they can see for themselves. At that moment I watch the trainee more than the screen. I'm looking for the slow nod as they accept that this new acted self is viable for their sense of who they are. Their comfort threshold has shifted. Their boundaries are expanding.

Reality follows fantasy.

Your own wording?

Specific act-as-if performance keys others have chosen:

    Act it!   It's show time!
    They love your act!   You're (…name of person…)!

🔑 5   HAVE FUN!
Alternatives: Enjoy their company! Take pleasure in their company! Warm to them!

You may be sceptical about the idea: *You can't pretend what you don't feel. You'll just end up with a false smile.* Well, yes, we've all seen such presenters and it's not a pretty sight; the smile looks as if it will only be removed with surgery. It's uncomfortable for everyone and, at best, we feel pity.

So pretence is out.

But what if you could make the real thing happen? That's a big question because it defies the traditional Western notion that feelings just happen to you—that you cannot create them at will. You can. Not directly, but by deliberately, in advance, adopting an attitude of fun.

Whoa. Won't fun be out of place for a work situation?

No, I'm not talking about putting on a clown suit here. But try this way of thinking about it:: enjoy the company of the audience.

Wouldn't even that be inappropriate for some topics?

No. The fun and enjoyment I'm talking about might or might not produce a smile with the mouth, depending on the topic. This kind of fun and enjoyment shows up mostly in the eyes. You can deliberately choose that attitude in advance. I have seen this performance key free presenters from the prison of their own worries.

Even so, we're skirting around the real point, which is known, subconsciously, by every individual in the room. Yet it is never spoken about in our hard-nosed work-places, even though the toughest individuals in the room cannot help but be affected by it.

The audience will genuinely enjoy being with you
as much as you genuinely enjoy being with them

Remember Nicola's story? (see p3). The insight of that extraordinary five-year-old taught me just how deeply we are drawn to people who like us and enjoy being with us.

If you really like people, you will have fun with them, warmly enjoying them, taking pleasure in their company. It won't be forced or false. You'll be relaxed in their presence, responsive, spontaneous. Those who really get this idea develop a sparkle in their eye that does not get turned on and off at the

78 How do I work out my personal performance key?

door—because it is a sparkle for all seasons. I have seen funeral speakers talk, with that sparkle, of the death of a loved one; and the whole assembly feels lifted.

Are you ambitious? Do you aspire to leadership? In that case, you can't afford to switch off your enjoyment of the people you're with just because they gather together as an audience.

In my youth, there was a music band called *Banish Misfortune*. This performance key banishes fear.

try this... Imagine that you're sitting with other staff, watching yourself speak. It's not a pleasant experience because that version of you is way too serious. Sure, the topic is serious, but does he have to look as if he was woken by the undertaker? His face is impassive, devoid of warmth. He's wrapped up in herself, worried about finding the right words, and even when he glances at people, he's not really seeing them. He doesn't want to be here. He doesn't want to be with you. Around you, the faces of the rest of the audience are draining of warmth. Their eyes are glazing over.

But he is you. So, enough of that. You tap him on the shoulder and take his place. You decide to have fun, to enjoy the audience, to take pleasure in their company. The change is dramatic. Your eyes sparkle. The natural enthusiasm for your topic comes back. You make your points strongly, often emphatically. The audience literally sits up straighter. Some start to ask interested questions, which you answer with enthusiasm. It's obvious to them that you're not just enjoying being here, you're enjoying them. You see on their faces little nods of appreciation. Their eyes warm to you.

Imagine the reality shift until the reality shifts.

Your own wording?

Specific decide-to-have-fun performance keys others have chosen:

    Good company!   Warm to them!
    Throw away the mask!   They're your mates!
    Party time!   Let the games begin!

 How do I become more persuasive and convincing?

Build rapport right at the beginning

Start with a genuine greeting.

How often we hear the opposite. The speaker opens in a flat tone:

"Good evening. I would like to express my sincere thanks for…"

Good evening? No. If you talk with the tonal equivalent of a flat tyre you're not wishing me a good evening at all. Sincere thanks? No. If you're sincere, you don't have to tell me you're sincere.

"…this opportunity to speak to you and to say what a pleasure it is…"

Pleasure? There is not a drop of pleasure in your tone. You're not glad to see me, so I'm not glad to see you.

We don't do it to individuals, so why do we do it to an audience? If you do genuinely feel warm about meeting and greeting an audience, it must be in your tone as well as your words. Say it 'like you mean it'.

Then, interact with the audience as soon as possible. For most speakers early interaction helps themselves as much as the audience. Speaker and audience swiftly find each other's wavelength, initial awkwardness and tensions vanish. Genuine warmth often comes into the speaker's eyes and he or she is instantly more natural.

Smaller audiences

Use someone's name.	"I shouldn't tell you this. Dale will have it in the social club newsletter before the end of tea break..."
Ask an open ended question and expect an answer. You may have to look around with raised eyebrows	"I know some of you have avoided taking on new staff so far. Why's that?"

Larger audiences

Ask a question and expect an answer. You may have to ask for a show of hands. Then comment on the response.	"'Morning everyone. How many of you were expecting the new appointments before the end of the year? Can you give me a show of hands…? Okay, thank you. Well in your shoes I would be expecting…"

Avoid rhetorical questions unless you're giving a high-drama, high-oratory speech. And even then, they have to be very well judged to reflect the emotional potential of the audience.

Signpost your presentation

Some speakers are so entertaining that the audience will luxuriate in the detail, suspending their desire for a sense of structure. But if it's not pure entertainment, your audience will want signposts—telling them where you are in the presentation.
  Examples:
"Now, the sales figures."
"As you'll see later..."
"Remember I told you that (….) Well, here's the pay-off..."
"And that's not the only cause of death in indoor plants…"
"That's enough on the effects of arachnophobia... now the cure."

Give them variety

"Take 'em by surprise." *British MP Barbara Castle.*

That was her advice to would-be speakers. It's what variety is about—surprising the audience, keeping them slightly off balance, not just with your content, but with your voice and body.
  Variety is usually more important than having a good energy level. Some public speakers are so energized you expect them to do handsprings and scorch the walls. And, for the first few minutes, the speaker may have you riveted; but if he stays a ball of fire, you will power down your message receptors and hope that someone will bring a hose to put him out.

> Audience insatiable desire: "Give me variety."

That means variety in all these: speed, tone, pitch, volume, intensity, body language, emphasis, silence. But don't try to remember a list like that, it's much better to develop a 'surprise 'em' frame of mind. Car passengers can sleep on a smooth or a rough road as long as the smoothness *or* roughness is constant. They can't sleep if the ride is unpredictable.

Which brings me to blirting.

Improve your persuasiveness by blirting

Yes, the spelling is correct. Blirting means suddenly increasing your pace. The word blirt is a horribly contrived acronym: Brief Loquacious & Interpersonal Responsiveness Test—a joke, of course, but it comes from a serious study at the University of Texas in 2002. The study found that if you suddenly increase your pace (and, we can assume, your sense of urgency), people perceive you as more persuasive, more authoritative, more likeable, and on top of things.

However, it's not the new pace that impresses as much as the change to the new pace. Variety is the priority. So you can slow up again. In fact, if you're planning to be a repeat blirter, slowing up between blirts might be a very good idea.

How to handle embarrassing mistakes

We've all suffered it. You make a mistake and the fastest lava flow in the world pours up your body and sets fire to your neck and head. Worse, many people prone to blushing are convinced that it's a permanent affliction. It doesn't have to be. The solution starts with an attitude you decide a long way in advance of mistakes.

First, realize its almost never the mistake that destroys your speak cred—it's your embarrassment. Audiences forgive mistakes quickly. They don't easily forgive embarrassment which makes them feel uncomfortable, and is perceived as a far greater sign of weakness than the mistake. So the long term answer starts with a decision you can make right away.

> Choose to be unembarrassable.

Yes, even embarrassment is a matter of choice.

My father told me of an incident on an Egyptian beach in the Second World War. Many soldiers were there on R & R. Local Egyptians were there also, including a young, rather aristocratic-looking woman. She was knocked down by a wave which neatly removed her upper clothing. Now what would you expect from soldiers on R & R. Cat calls? Crude jeering? Whistles? No. The woman stood, retrieved her clothing and donned it with such poise and dignity that, to a man, every soldier stood and applauded as she left the beach.

It's not what happens that matters, it's how you handle what happens. Embarrassment works like fear. If you don't feel embarrassed, there is nothing to be embarrassed about.

What if I blush easily? I don't have a choice over that, surely.

Yes you do. You begin with that long term decision to be unembarrassable, but there are two more things you can do on the spot when things go wrong.

First:

Share their enjoyment. Laugh with them.

- Be open with the audience about what's happening. If that means admitting a mistake, do so matter-of-factly, knowing that in the long term you are much bigger than any one error.

- Laugh with the audience. It could be anything from a wouldn't-you-know-it smile to laughing out loud at yourself.

- After a pause for the merriment to die down, resume with your original demeanour.

An example: a manager in my home town farewelled an old colleague in front of 200 watersiders, a deeply cynical and formidable audience, easily capable of humiliating any 'stuffed-shirt' management presenter. Even though that colleague had been a personal friend for decades, the manager forgot his name at the crucial moment. So he turned with a calm but wry smile to the watersiders and said, "You know, I've known this guy for 25 years and do you think I can remember his name now?" The watersiders roared with laughter, laughing *with* him.

How different that would have been if he had stuttered and stammered and tried to cover up.

I've left the best to last. It's short, it's simple and it's deep. If you take to it, you won't need the previous tips. Adopt this attitude:

An audience can see right through me, faults and all,
and that's okay.

That can look daunting until you know that it represents real strength, not weakness. And it's not the defiant strength that doesn't 'give-a-damn' what anyone thinks; it's the much more convincing strength that is completely relaxed about exposed human flaws. In any case, guess what audiences dislike more than anything—not what they might see in you, but your fear of what they might see in you. It's time to get over that fear. It's okay to be seen for what you are.

Can you also see what relief, relaxation and exhilaration could come from adopting that attitude?

Be open, but not an open book

I'm not talking about telling the truth or lying. By openness, I mean acknowledging what's happening at the factual and the emotional level.

- *Acknowledge opposition.* If your argument is going to be opposed by others, acknowledge the opposing argument. If there's likely to be a negative feeling about your argument, acknowledge the feeling.

- *Don't pretend knowledge you don't have.* Consciously or subconsciously, an audience knows. Even an audience that doesn't consciously decide you're faking will feel uneasy.

- *Do admit your mistakes.* Never with embarrassment or humility, always with matter-of-fact acknowledgement. You are bigger than your mistakes. (See also *How to handle audience anger when you deserve it* p114.)

However, make sure you are only open on subjects that flow naturally out of the topic or the needs of the audience that day. We all want to be liked by an audience, that's perfectly natural. But if that want is too strong, it can become a need. When we need to be liked, we're tempted to reveal unrelated personal details about ourselves, and that will come across as naïve or ingratiating.

When your personal views conflict with your message

Your employer expects you to give a message you disagree with. How you handle that depends on whether your audience is internal or external.

The manager and the internal audience

Let's say your job is to get the despatch and delivery staff in behind the new trucking schedule which, in theory, is going to reduce costs and raise profits. Personally, you think the new schedule is a disaster. You made your feelings plain at the planning stage, but you were over-ruled.

In the middle of your presentation, one of the delivery staff asks, "Yes, but what's your personal view? Isn't this going to back-fire on us?"

There's the dilemma. The mental dialogue is *If I'm honest I betray the company I work for. If I lie, I betray myself and my staff.* The most immediate temptation is probably the bare-faced lie, "Yes, I think it'll work." But all that does is announce the death of your personal credibility, and should reap words from the CEO about misguided loyalty.

What about this response? "I wouldn't tell you that one way or the other, because I'm not here to give my personal view." But that doesn't work either, because to the staff you can't be simply a title and a non-person. They'll see it as a cover up and again you'll lose personal credibility.

The key to the answer is the audience—they, too, are the company and a company that lies to itself is sick.

For an internal audience, be constructively honest, revealing your personal opinions when asked.

You might use language like this: "Personally, I've had reservations. But I was a lone voice on it and this policy has come out of days of weighing different arguments. Now that it's decided, we need to do our part to make sure that it works and works well." If questioned further about those reservations, explain that they are now irrelevant. If your company is foolish enough to criticize you for that approach, look for a healthier company.

However, there's honesty, and then there's honesty delivered with a baseball bat. If any manager of mine were to answer, "Well, now that you ask, I think it's a load of weasel droppings," we would probably have a discussion about his future.

The manager and the external audience

This time we have to draw a line between honesty and revealing personal opinions. When you represent your organization externally, you owe strangers honesty but not personal disclosures. The line may be hard to draw, depending on to what extent you are in front of the external audience as yourself and to what extent as a manager. If you're there predominantly to represent your organization, here's the rule:

> For an external audience, be constructively honest *without* revealing personal opinions.

Now, the sentence we tried and rejected above, has a chance of working. Say it lightly and dismissively: "Oh no, I wouldn't tell you that one way or the other, because I'm here to represent my company, not to give my personal view." It works only if the company hat is the only one on your head. And even then it only works up to a point. In spite of the phrase 'one way or the other', it may still sound like a face-saver. Your tone will carry it as long as it implies *Good grief no, it would be most inappropriate to give my personal opinion when I'm here representing my company.* In some situations, that last thought might work said out loud.

Keep your body language open

When you perform well, your body language implies, *I'm happy to be seen, known and understood by you.* At least one hand should be out of a pocket and free to gesture. Almost always, your movements and gestures should take your arms away from your body, particularly away from your chest. Don't allow your hands to join constantly, either in front or behind. Hand-wringing or hand-washing movements are definitely wrong.

Of course, when we're performing well (in 'flow'), we don't consciously think about our body language at all. But every now and then, even experienced speakers are suddenly, uncomfortably, aware of what their bodies are doing. If that's happening to you, then the solution is to temporarily adopt a 'home' stance—that's a relaxed body position in which you could speak for a minute without moving from the spot.

> **try this...**
>
> *Work out your own home stance*
> No single stance works for everyone, but there are a couple of rules.
>
> If you're standing, the home stance should be asymmetric—and just putting your weight on one leg may be all that's needed. Also, as I just mentioned, your hands should not be clasped together. Get a friend to tell you if you look comfortable and relaxed. You continue to speak in this stance, without moving your feet, until you know you can return your full focus to topic and audience. Then let the home stance go and allow normal movement to resume.
>
> For a sitting home stance, most people are comfortable with this: put your backside in the back of the seat and incline forward so that your forearms can rest on the table. You can have your hands touching, but only lightly so that one hand can easily lift away and gesture.
>
> Standing or sitting, the home stance must feel natural for you—so natural that you will soon forget to think about your body and return to flow.

For informal occasions, here's a useful trick, mostly for men. Start with one hand, or just a thumb, in a trouser pocket. Use the other hand for emphasis, pulling out the first hand when you need it. Once you get into the flow, you'll find you don't need to return to the pocket. For women without pockets, try holding a small object like a pen to get you started, putting it down when you're under way. Don't click the pen.

As for meaningful gestures to the audience, be sure that the gesture is suitable, especially in these days of mixed culture audiences. The first man on the moon, Neil Armstrong, closed thumb and index finger and sent the televised gesture earthwards. He meant *everything's okay*, but millions in eastern Europe thought he was telling them *you are an orifice at the south end of the alimentary canal*.

Look at everyone with your chest

That's another way of saying don't just swivel your eyeballs. Nor is it enough to turn your head. Your whole upper body has to move, signalling *I am open to you*. And you. And you. That doesn't mean that you turn your chest absolutely square on to each person you look at—that would be robotic—but it should turn at least part of the way, even when you're sitting.

Move only your eyes and people will trust you about as much as they trust a snake in dark glasses.

Sitting presenters—sit up

We've all seen variations on this movie scene: Sheriff Matt Ozick Jr. is in his office, relaxing, feet crossed and on the table, Budweiser at hand, six gallon hat pulled down over his forehead. The phone rings. Only his hand moves, lazily reaching for the receiver, just as lazily bringing it back to his ear.

"Yo," he says in a bored voice.

We can't hear the voice at the other end, but whatever it says has a remarkable effect on Sheriff Matt Ozick Jr. His eyes widen, his feet dive for the ground, he pulls his chair up to the desk, straightens his upper back and inclines slightly forward.

"Yes, Mr President," he says.

Straightens his upper back and inclines slightly forward? Yes, because instinctively we know that we perform better with that posture when we're sitting. Many people override that instinct with the false belief that we do better when we're relaxed. We don't. Eighty per cent of our air normally comes from full operation of the diaphragm. If we don't have a straight upper back, we can't operate the diaphragm properly and have little access to that eighty per cent.

The power of silence

Silence. It's one of the most powerful words in the English language. Beginners feel especially vulnerable during silences; so they desperately fill them with ums, and-ums and ahs, until the audience takes a siesta under the blanket of continuous sound. Experienced speakers are not just relaxed about silences, but deliberately inject them as part of giving their message impact. Yes, silence has as much impact as the best content, often more. Once you're comfortable with silence, you have a powerful tool at your disposal.

> The longer you can pause,
> the more personal authority you have,
> and the more status your audience will give you.

As he dismisses 3B, the maths teacher says, "I want to see Timkins, Smythe and Carruthers. The rest of you may go." Timkins, Smythe and Carruthers glance at each other fearfully and approach, wringing caps in hands and stand, white-faced, before him.

"Well, well, well," he says and looks slowly from one pair of petrified eyes to the next. In silence.
Carruthers and Timkins swallow simultaneously.
More silence.
"It wasn't my fault," squeaks Timkins. "They made me."
More silence. The maths teacher breathes in and he breathes out.
"I didn't," Carruthers blurts, "Timkins brought the matches. And Smythe lit it.'

Even if you don't want your audience to babble terrified confessions, never underestimate the power of silence for dramatic emphasis.

try this... Read each of the following lines aloud to a friend, asking that friend to pretend to be in the middle of an audience.

Read each without the pause, then with the pause. When you put in the pause, make it at least one second long and during that silence look from one place in your imaginary audience to another. For a larger audience, make that two seconds.

"If we can't cure our own dependence on drugs... (pause)... then when our children get hooked... (pause)... we have no-one to blame but ourselves."

OR

"Get this, lads... (pause)... Ignore this one simple precaution... (pause)... and you'll find yourself at 10,000 feet in a machine with the flying qualities of a brick."

OR

"You've been told that the government recognizes your equality... *(pause)...* you've been told that the law *guarantees* your equality... *(pause)...* you have even been told... *(pause)...* that you now *have* equality... *(pause)...* but we all know that if you want the top jobs you have to be better than equal!"

Feel the power of the pause?

Bigger audiences want *you* to be bigger

Yes, you as well as the visual aids. The bigger the audience, the more these points are true:

- Increase your energy. (Includes volume, but is more than volume)
- Raise your average pitch (higher voice) as you would if you were calling out to someone a distance away. Increase the whole pitch range of your voice (higher ups and lower downs).

- Lengthen your pauses significantly. Pauses are always important, but in a large audience they become vital. A large audience cannot easily hear wall-to-wall words and is quickly bored.

- Exaggerate your gestures and expressions. Frown deeper, smile wider, raise eyebrows higher. For a very big audience, raising eyebrows may well mean spreading your arms.

But what if I have a microphone?
The surprise is that no matter how good your microphone and sound system, all of those points above are still true. A microphone does nothing but raise your volume. Next time you see a presenter talking to a very large audience, watch how much they work the energy, pitch and range of their voice. They speak almost as if the sound system was not working. (For more see p43).

Your notes and the lectern

Keep half a pace back from the lectern, so that when you drop your eyes to your notes, you don't have to drop your head. If you have more than one page, slide the pages, don't turn them.

Many speakers need a lectern for security. Some need it so badly they take a death grip on it—you can see their knuckles go white—and I have even seen terrified speakers rock the lectern in different directions. That's the lectern tango. It must be tempting for some in the audience to call out and ask if they can reserve the last dance.

> Terminate the lectern tango

Yes. It is better to come on out from behind; it's part of the openness we talked about earlier. But many find it difficult to abandon the security. Also, having ventured out, there's often a problem with referring back to notes left on the lectern. At first, the prospect of such a long trip, especially in silence, can be terrifying. Many trainees are convinced only when they see themselves do it on a video re-play.

Don't come away from the lectern until you know you're on a comfortable roll with your words and can speak spontaneously for a minute or two.

Now, do you need to check your notes?

- Stop speaking while your eyes are still on the audience.

- Break eye contact with the audience.
- Walk back to the lectern, get the prompt, start walking out again.
- Make eye contact with the audience.
- Speak again.

The audience not only copes with such silence, they want it. The bigger the audience, the bigger the pause they want and the more status they'll award you for doing it. However, like any movement, it mustn't become frequent and predictable. If you need a lot of prompting you had better carry your notes with you, or stay behind the lectern.

Tell stories to make your message memorable

An example: a first aid instructor is trying to impress her students with the fact that rescuers are sometimes more likely to react to blood than the victims themselves. If she told the principle it would sound like this:

> "You'll find sometimes that you'll react to blood more than the victim does. If you don't guard against it, you could endanger the lives of the people you're trying to help."

Compare the effectiveness of that approach, with this:

> "In 1931, early in the morning of December 14th, an air ace called Douglas Bader cart-wheeled his plane along the runway. When the wreckage came to a halt, Bader sat there in what was left of the cockpit, critically injured. Men rushed out from the clubhouse, including the steward who had the foresight to bring brandy from the bar.
> "'Here you are, sir,' said the steward. 'Have this brandy.'
> "'No, thanks very much,' said Douglas Bader. 'I don't drink.'
> "The steward leaned over to urge him, saw the blood spurting, turned ashen, then stood back and drank the brandy himself.
> "The point is this, you'll find sometimes that you'll react to blood more than the victim does. If you don't guard against it..."

Which way makes the message memorable?

Use colourful comparisons

Example: she went through that property faster than a cat through a dog pound.

Get personal. Give your stories stars

Example: "On a sunny day in 1914, a young man called Rupert Turner put on his tweed jacket, polished his teeth with a used handkerchief, and strolled down to the local strip club..."

Get detailed, get particular

Not, "Harold was in a bad mood yesterday." Instead, "Yesterday morning, Harold wakes up. The first thing he sees is the cracked plaster on the ceiling. The first thing he thinks is that there's no food in the cupboard. And the first thing he tastes is what's left on his tongue from the night before. Or was it two nights? He's not sure."

Become a painter

Have you noticed how the examples above put pictures in your head?

Persuasive people paint pictures with words

Mario Cuomo, ex Mayor of New York, is one of the world's better speakers. At a Democratic convention he laid a whip into the Republicans with this word picture gem.

> "The Republicans believe that the wagon train will not make it to the frontier, unless some of the old, some of the young, some of the weak, are left behind by the side of the road. The strong, they tell us, will inherit the land. We Democrats believe something else. We Democrats believe that we can make it all the way with the whole family intact!"

Here's one of the most effective uses of word pictures I know. Some years back, an American man left his wife and children for another woman. He maintained contact with his family, but didn't seem to understand the distress and suffering they were going through. His small daughter set out to try to make him understand—with this word picture.

"Dear Dad. I had a dream about Mum and me and Tina. We was driving along the road in the car. Mum was driving pretty good with us kids sitting in the back. We was laughing and telling jokes and Mum was laughing too. Then a huge big truck came roaring out of a yard and hit us in the side. The car was totalled, but we weren't killed. We went to hospital for a long time. After that we didn't want to do anything much and we just stayed home. But then we came outside and started playing again okay and we started playing with our friends again. Mum walked everywhere for a while. But it was too far so she got another car. She couldn't drive it at first, but then she started to and she could drive to the supermarket and back okay. Dad, in my dream you were the driver of the truck."

Illustrative, relevant stories convince and persuade.

Make humour work for you

It's commonly said that humour boosts the audience's ability to remember by 20 per cent. Regardless of the figure, humour is a sharp tool to have on your belt, as long as you follow a few rules.

- Make it relevant. The best jokes are an extension of your message. An isolated, unrelated joke is very difficult to run successfully. (See also *Tell an anecdote* p32)

- Rehearse it: word-for-word. For once I'm only suggesting spontaneity if you're an experienced stand-up comedian.

Now I'm going to break the eleventh commandment: Thou shalt not analyse a joke.

Telling the essence of a joke is usually not funny. Most of the humour is in how you put the joke together. In this example, read all the way down the left-hand column first, before you look at the commentary on the right.

...the fact is we we've been very, very lucky. We were in the right place at the right time. Our toast has fallen jammy side up.	The link. Making the imminent humour relevant.

How do I become more persuasive and convincing? 93

Which reminds me of the little old Jewish tailor who lived in a remote village in the depths of Germany.	*Little, old, remote village, depths.* Paint specific, detailed pictures with your words.
One day he put down his needle, made himself a slice of bread and jam and was just about to take his first bite...	*One day.* The storyteller mode. The child in all of us feels pleasure in hearing it.
...when it fell on the floor—jammy side up! He was astounded.	*Jammy... side... up!.* Emphasis. Your whole body should be involved in astonishment.
He said to himself, "I am a Jew. In Germany. How can I have so much luck?"	Act it. Spread your hands, raise your eyebrows. The same sequence is delivered three times, building tension, and reinforcing what has to be understood for the punch-line to be funny.
He went to the village elders and told them how the bread had fallen jammy side up. He said, "I am a Jew. In Germany. How can I have so much luck?" And they were astonished.	
They spent days, puzzling over the problem.	Act it. Building tension.
They consulted amongst themselves, they consulted the ancient writings of the Torah, they consulted God.	This powerful pattern of three phrases is known as the Rule of Three. It's important not to rush it.
Then they went back to the little old tailor and said, "We have the answer."	
The tailor put down his needle. What is it?" he asked. "I am a Jew. In Germany. How can I have so much luck?".	Builds more tension. The elders don't just arrive and deliver the answer.
And they said, "It is because you put your jam on the wrong side of the bread!"	Never put 'they said' last. The punch line is right at the end, with high energy to ram it home.

94 How do I become more persuasive and convincing?

> When preparing humour, add words that build visual pictures and heighten tension, remove words that don't.

One more point. Don't pussy-foot your way into a joke with 'Stop me if you've heard this one' or 'I hope you haven't heard this one'. Head straight into it. Take the risk. If someone finishes your punch line for you, he will come back as a spotted toad in the next life.

Abuse the audience

One of the most successful forms of humour is to bend a joke so you can abuse your audience. In the West, audiences love to be abused. Why else would we have *Faulty Towers* restaurants where customers pay exorbitantly for actor/waiters to treat them like rubbish that just blew in off the alley? It works well, as long as you follow two rules:

- It must be witty.
- It must be obviously outrageous or absurdly exaggerated.

If it's not, you could belittle someone; the laughter will be brittle and the audience will lower it's estimation of you even as it laughs.

Examples: (To a group of surgeons) But then what else can you expect? He's a surgeon. He suffers from love bites... most of them self-inflicted. (To lawyers) It's a terrible mistake to insult a lawyer. I did it once and he was so angry he was beside himself... you never saw such an unattractive couple. (To a group of public speakers) Yes, like all public speakers he's a dedicated exhibitionist. In the winter he jumps out in front of girls and describes himself.

Take advantage of inherent humour

You don't plan inherent humour, you take advantage of whatever happens or is said. It's not as side-splitting as a carefully crafted joke, but it's usually the most heart-warming humour. It's gentle, it brings chuckles, here and there, along with audience rapport.

For inherent humour you don't have to be a born comedian. It's easily learned if you practise spotting and exploiting opportunities, not just in presentations but in everyday conversations. Some get a good start, growing up in families that encourage such opportunism. I didn't have that start, but

I've learned it and it's one of the skills I value most. When inherent humour knocks, let it in.

Take advantage of the inherent humour of an event by exaggerating it to the point of absurdity.

An example: someone from the audience knocks over a glass and spills ice and water in his neighbour's lap. Do you say, Would you like me to stop a moment while you clean up? No, you exploit the inherent humour: "If you thought he needed a shower, you could have just said!"

Another: you've just told the audience, "...and never, ever, force cats to perform in front a camera. They feel the tension..." But why stop there? Exploit the inherent humour by extending the concept into the absurd. "I'm telling you, if you force a cat to perform it will take your hand off at the elbow!" Or you could play-act the cat-to-human conversation, looking each way at the right time.

"I don't want to."
"Yes you do."
"I don't *want* to..."
"You'll love it. You know you will."
"I'm *warning* you..." Inherent humour doesn't demand a perfect punch line or a born comedian. Let your imagination go a little more each time; it will get easier and you will get funnier.

Signals to journalists

If you've been in an audience with a television crew videoing the speaker you may have noticed a curious pantomime. If the speaker is working without notes, or departing from speech notes, the reporter probably looks intensely focused. He'll be fixated on the speaker, eyes narrowed, listening for pearls amongst the words. Every now and then he'll tap the camera operator on the leg and the red light will come on, usually half-way through a sentence. Another tap, it goes off.

But if the speaker is experienced, the reporter may look considerably more relaxed. When the speaker comes to the part he knows is going to be important, he'll put out a media signpost. : "And let me tell you this... (pause, reporter taps camera operator, red light goes on)..." or "And I can't stress this enough... (pause)..."

It doesn't matter which medium we're talking about—internet, print, radio or television—all journalists will take notice, even though they know exactly what you're doing. They know that what you see as important might well be what the public sees as interesting.

How to apologize or admit a mistake

> "When you say 'I'm sorry', look the person in the eye."
> *From a Nepalese tantra.*

In this case, it's the audience you look in the eye.

It used to be normal for private and public organisations to see an apology or admission of fault as a credibility catastrophe. Individual managers and executives thought that if they owned up in front of an audience, their personal authority would automatically go into free fall. It's a sign of a maturing society that that view is changing. You can be genuinely sorry, you can admit error and apologize, in such a way that your personal authority goes up—if you follow a few simple rules.

For small mistakes with no consequence

Simply come on out with it—own up or apologize or both—and mean it. No fuss, no drama, no embarrassment. You are bigger than one mistake. A wry smile at yourself is as worked up as you get before you move on.

For larger mistakes with significant consequences

> Use the three Rs: Regret, Restitution, Reform, acknowledging the feelings of those affected.

Show that you regret the mistake, say how you're going to put it right for the people affected, and say what you are doing to lessen the chance that it will happen again. (That pattern works just as well in a media interview. For that, you first need to make your peace with the CEO, the insurance representative, the company lawyer, and your External Communications Manager. I have seen some interesting shouting matches.)

Has your mistake put people out? Are they annoyed or angry? If so, then in the first part—regret—you will also need to acknowledge those feelings.

Now. It's all very well following a formula, but there are two vital elements you can't put in a formula. First, be genuinely sorry. Second, don't beat yourself up. That's not a contradiction. If you wear indignity—humility, embarrassment, or any kind of sackcloth and ashes—you'll embarrass the audience and they're likely to take longer to forgive that than the original mistake. Even an audience that is angry with you and panting for an apology, wants you to behave with dignity. You are bigger than any mistake and your fundamental character is not threatened.

...I'm so sorry. I completely misjudged the situation...	**Regret.** Genuine regret expressed in a dignified way.
	If you want more formality, for a more serious mistake, "I want to offer you my apologies for..."
...I know it must have been annoying to have to fork out of your own pockets to pay for it.	Acknowledging the feelings of those affected. This is often the key moment when the audience decides if your apology is sincere. Trust is renewed.
Of course you'll get that back. I'll be contacting everyone affected over the next few days.	**Restitution.** What you're doing to make it right for the people affected.
And we can't have something like this happening again. Leslie and I will be drawing up a plan for how to handle it if we ever have such a challenge again.	**Reform.** What you're doing to lessen the chance of a repeat.

A final tip. No sincere apology needs the word sincere. To say, "I want to offer you my sincere apologies," is about as convincing as telling the audience how honest you are and how much they can trust you.

Never, ever, apologize for your speaking abilities

> "Why don't the feller who says, 'I'm not a speech maker' let it go at that instead o' givin' a demonstration." *Kin Hubbard.*

98 How do I become more persuasive and convincing?

Most of us groan internally when we hear a speaker apologize for his shortcomings in advance. Why do we dislike it? Because the real message is: *I want to lower your expectations so that you'll judge me by an easier standard. I don't want you to feel let down at the end, so I'll do it now.* It's also a submission signal, *Please don't think badly of me,* and a self-fulfilling prophecy.

Speak the language of real people

> "Nothing gets in the way of doing business more than language that is anything other than conversational."
> *The Articulate Executive, Granville N. Toogood.*

We've all seen it. The presenter may well intend to say: "Thank you for this chance to explain what my project team has been up to." Instead his tongue breaks into an alien language: "I would like to express my sincere appreciation and that of my partner for your generosity in allowing me this opportunity to address the topic of the projected and actual outcomes of the project carried out by the team I am currently privileged to facilitate."

Who needs sleeping pills when you could listen to that? Next time you suspect yourself of delivering the language of the little green men, ask yourself this:

The corridor question:

How would I say this
if I met just one of these people in the corridor?

That question alone can transform speeches from detached, stuffy and jargon-filled to simple, personal, and direct. The corridor question is an outrageously simple and effective idea.

Sometimes I meet an objection.

Jack is a government department official. He's in front of a group of fellow officials, practicing a forthcoming speech to a public audience. I start the camera, the red light winks on and he begins.

"Good afternoon, ladies and gentlemen. At this point in time I would like to assure present members of the public that a multi-faceted, multi-level monitoring system is being maintained by the department with the express purpose of dealing with complaints, and indeed with any complainant who has indicated dissatisfaction." Already half the audience are glassy-eyed and losing muscle tone, but Jack soldiers on. "Indeed it has necessitated a re-evaluation of the service so as to maximize efficiency, and in so doing, significantly improve—".

"Wait, wait." I kill the red light. Throughout the audience, arms hang lifelessly down the sides of the chairs. One man's head has fallen back in the fly-catching position. I play the tape back to Jack.

"You hear how many very long sentences and formal words you're using?"

"Of course. But this is important material."

And there's the problem. Jack, like many, believes that if the topic or occasion is important it must be matched with the Language Of Importance. He is sceptical when his colleagues suggest that he ease up on the long words. Then he says something genuinely but mistakenly felt by many officials, especially in public service. "If I talk in ordinary language, it will sound unimportant, the topic will lose impact and I'll lose credibility."

There's only one thing for it: the corridor question.

"Jack, imagine that you met one of the public out there in the corridor and you used that language on him. What would he think?"

"He'd think I've got screws that need tightening. But I wouldn't do it to one person. This is an audience. It's different."

No it isn't.

Every individual wants you to speak
in the same conversational language you would use
if you were talking to him or her alone.

The corridor concept has limits and exceptions, of course. Obviously you will have to leave out the extremely casual remarks and crude language. Also, there are some formal social occasions where you must use the Language Of Importance or the audience will feel short-changed (see *Formal or special occasions* p125). Not many young couples would thank the minister for saying, "Consider yourselves hitched. Okay, start smooching."

But for almost all work-related occasions, your credibility with an audience has nothing to do with the Language Of Importance and everything to do with the language of real people.

You must, of course, be real to yourself. Some speakers falsely adopt the colloquialisms of their audience in an effort to get on their side. It's a terrible mistake. The falseness is instantly transparent and audiences promptly award a credibility rating of zero. The language of real people is your own, in its simplest, plainest, most direct and unaffected form. Here's a little tool to help you put the concept into practice.

Use the words 'you' or 'we' to an audience
as if talking to a single person.

An example. Imagine that you're sitting with 100 other staff, listening to an address from the CEO. Imagine that the CEO says to you all, "All staff are asked to make every effort to clarify their project preferences, and to submit their intentions to the office at the earliest opportunity. The company will endeavour to co-operate with those requests."

As a staff member, how well would you relate to that?

But what if the CEO said it like this? "Please decide which project you want, then tell the office staff as soon as you can. We'll do our best to make it happen for you."

Of the two CEO's, which do you relate to best? Which has the greatest personal authority in front of an audience? Which is most likely to get your cooperation, now and in the future? Which one best answers the corridor question?

All answers should be the same.

# How do I handle questions and interjections?

The sharing technique. How to handle even the toughest audience interaction with ease and authority

I salute the comedian Jerry Seinfeld who was talking to a live audience when someone called out, "Jerry, I love you."

"And I love you," he called back. "But I want to go on seeing other people."

The laughter and applause was, of course, for his wit. But mixed into that response was admiration for that demonstration of personal authority—that's both connected and separate personal authority. He was fully engaged and comfortable with his audience, not the least bit threatened or upset by the interruption.

What's your feeling about interruptions? Do you dislike them or welcome them? What about emotionally charged expressions of disapproval of your message? Do you hate them, or do you—and this is the aim—welcome even these?

The technique in this chapter is one of the finest ways of developing your personal authority, and it's particularly good for building rapport with an audience, even when your message is unwelcome. It will help you handle virtually any kind of unexpected event, including questions, interjections, cross-fire amongst the audience, aggressive comments about your message, hostility and personal attacks on you. It even works for handling attacks on you when you deserve it.

Here's a summary in advance.

THE ATTITUDE	Listen on behalf of everyone
THE CORE TECHNIQUE	Share the reply, showing warmth, interest and energy
HANDLING FEELINGS	Accept the feelings, argue the facts

THE ATTITUDE
Listen on behalf of everyone

Some presenters fear questions and interjections even more than they fear one-way speaking. Allowing something unexpected to happen feels like opening Pandora's box and releasing all manner of unknown horrors. So this kind of self-talk switches on.

"Excuse me."
Uh oh. "Yes?"
"I have a question."
Oh no. A question. It'll put me off my stride. It'll put me off what I prepared. What if I don't know the answer? I'll look like a fool.

That self-talk is a destroyer because it shunts your focus right back on your worries. Your fears multiply, your audience knows instantly that you've transferred interest from them to you, and your credibility takes a hammering before you've uttered two words of your response.

Instead, develop self-talk like this: *Ah, good. Chances are others will have the same question and this helps me understand how others in the audience feel. How can I use this to help everyone understand?* Make that your self-talk even when the questions and interjections are probing or emotionally charged.

Decide to genuinely welcome questions and interjections

That's quite a decision, because you have to mean it. But once you do, you'll find yourself easily coping with that instant when you don't know what your response is going to be.

Imagine yourself at a party. You're talking to one person, a glass of your favourite lubricant at hand. But you're not enjoying it because the person opposite you is boring. Which is a puzzle because he has an interesting background, he's done spectacular things and he's extremely well-informed. So how can he be boring? Feelings and judgements like *boring* or *arrogant* or *I don't like this bozo* often arise when the person in front of us keeps talking with no sign that he wants to know about us.

It's the same when a presenter doesn't want to know about our concerns.

Listen on behalf of the audience. You're there for them.

Let's get a practical barrier out of the way. For a large audience, it just doesn't work to take every question and interjection as they arise, because you would never get through your message. It is better to have a stated question time. So, still welcome the questions, but manage their timing.

THE CORE TECHNIQUE
Share the reply, showing warmth, interest and energy

Let's do this in the order it happens. From the first moment of the question or interjection:

- Show warmth to the questioner.
- Show interest in the question.
- Add energy to the reply.

Show warmth. In that split second when you realize that someone wants to interrupt with a question or interjection, your personal authority is on the line. If your first reaction is apprehensive, your audience cools; if you are warm, your audience warms to you. Don't overdo it. Be warm with your eyes only—this is not the place for a cheesy smile.

Show interest. Immediately—almost simultaneously with the warmth—show interest in what's being put to you. Your expression must indicate that you really want to know what's going on for this person. Being genuinely interested conveys respect for the question and questioner.

But what if I don't have a ready answer?

If you need time to think of the answer,
nod to the questioner, look away and think,
in silence.

What? Then they'll know I don't know the answer!

Exactly. That's the reality and there's just no convincing way to pretend otherwise. But it's only a problem if you make it so. Besides, the audience doesn't mind if you think for a few seconds; by thinking in silence, you convey more respect for the question and the questioner. Of course, if you're embarrassed, all bets are off. Audiences hate that.

Here's a challenge: see if you can convey your interest in the question without saying, "That's a good question," which usually means *I'm buying time while I try to think of an answer*. It can also mean *Please go away and die*. At best, "That's a good question" is a value judgement and the audience doesn't appreciate it unless you mean it so sincerely your eyes sparkle with appreciation.

Add energy. As you begin your response, be slightly energized by the question or interjection, right from the first word of your response. That means a slight increase in volume and intensity, eyebrows slightly higher. Being energized by a question or interjection also conveys respect. The opposite is a disaster; some presenters are so reluctant to take questions and interjections, they drop their energy. That conveys: *your interruption is not important and I want to get it out of the way quickly. It's a nuisance. Go away.* Not much respect in that; it would be simpler to stroll over and slap the questioner in the face.

As you improve at genuine warmth, interest and energy, you'll find it easier to find the words for a reply.

Now, share that reply. The entire technique centres on the shared reply.

- Deliver only the first phrase to the questioner.

- Deliver the rest to the entire audience.

- Come back to finish on the questioner.

> It's rude to talk only to the person who asked the question or interjected.

Rude? Who to?

To the audience.

Doesn't it defy normal rules of courtesy? Weren't we all taught as youngsters to look at any adult asking us a question?

So we were, but for group communication that rule breaks down. The group psychology is that when someone asks a question (or interjects), the whole audience owns it. It's as if the entire group asked the question and wants to hear your response even when many already know the answer.

Still not convinced?

try this... A thought experiment: imagine you're in the front row of an audience of 200. You ask a question, but the answer is a long one and the presenter looks at you straight down the barrel for the entire time with everyone watching both of you. How do you feel? Uncomfortable, of course. You're likely to want to turn into a flatworm and exit under the carpet. And how does the rest of the audience feel? Impatient. Ignored. *Would you two like us to leave the room? Can we be part of this, or is it a private party for two?*

Now, ask yourself this. How small does the audience need to be in order to ignore this rule? That's right—one. The psychology applies to all audiences. It's not well known, because the vast majority of audiences are small, twenty people or less, and the effect less obvious. Most presenters 'lock on' to the questioner and get away with it. But that behaviour doesn't connect with the audience, so it's low on connected personal authority.

Most people need to try the sharing technique before they believe it.

try this... Persuade at least four friends or colleagues to help you out as a practice audience. Tell them what you're doing. Explain that you want someone to interrupt with a question (a 'how' or 'why' question is best) about half a minute after you start speaking. On the first run, deliberately do not share the reply—lock on to the questioner for the whole response. Now ask the questioner to repeat the same question. This time, share the reply as described above. Ask your audience which way looked best. Which way did you feel you had more control?

Re-gather the audience. When you turn away from the questioner, quickly round up the whole audience with your eyes. If, for example, the questioner is on the right hand side, your first look might be to the far left, then back to the far right, then randomly here and there. You're signalling the audience that this question is so interesting that every person in the room might be interested in the answer.

And remember that you must involve your upper body in looking around. (*Look at everyone with your chest* P89) Move you eyes only and it will be as if you're sitting there wearing a hood.

At the end of your response, return to nod thanks to the questioner. You might raise your eyebrows questioningly, or ask directly, "Have I answered your question?"

Back to warmth and interest. It applies to even the toughest and nastiest interjection. Why? Because you are there for your audience, not for your survival. This is fundamental respect at its best, not only for the interjector but also for others who have the same concerns.

In all following examples Y means You, Q means questioner or interjector. I suggest you read all of the left side before you look at the commentary on the right.

How do I handle questions and interjections?

Large group

We'll assume you've got an audience of, say, 100, where we can't be sure everyone heard the question. And we'll assume straight-forward questions, with no hidden agendas.

	INTERACTION	COMMENTARY
Y	"You have a question?"	Already you're showing warmth and interest.
Q	"Yes. Can you tell is if the Middle East situation is going to raise prices even further?"	
Y	"You mean at the pumps?"	You're wanting to fully understand before you reply
Q	"Yes."	
Y	*You nod, then turn to the rest of the audience.*	Looking away from the questioner is usually the most difficult part for beginners.
	"The question is, 'Will the Middle East situation raise petrol prices even further...	You're adding energy. Your whole manner indicates that this is an interesting question for all of us.'
	"I don't know yet. This may well be just another bump in a very bumpy, very long Middle East road. I'm reluctant to even guess about prices until I know what the OPEC nations have to say. Their opinion may be the best indicator anyone's going to get. *Return to questioner on last words, with nod of thanks*	
	"Which brings me to the local reaction..."	Moving your audience back to your agenda.

Now let's go to a much smaller group where it's so tempting to give the answer only to the questioner, one-to-one. This time, you're running a meeting with half a dozen people. Assume everyone heard the interjection.

How do I handle questions and interjections? 107

Small group

Y	"My feeling is that if we don't terminate her contract, the-"	
Q	"But, Miranda, she's a solo parent, disabled, and with three children under five. The press will make us roast of the day."	You're listening to this with warmth and interest, even though you were interrupted. This objection to your message is actually a gift, because it openly declares a feeling that might otherwise be hidden, silently undermining you.
Y	*You incline your head slightly forward.*	Take careful note of this movement. It's not a nod in the usual sense. The forward inclination indicates that you accept the contribution and the feeling behind it, but that you don't necessarily agree with the face value of the point made.
	"Yes, they will…	You're giving the first phrase only to the questioner. You're already energized by the unexpected interjection.
	You turn to the others.	Sharing the reply.
	"…but what's the alternative? She's blackmailing us with her disadvantaged status so she can go right on doing it to the same youngsters. The parents are going to get the press to roast us anyway.	Sustaining the added energy.

Returning to questioner to give nod of thanks. The supposedly negative objection was a gift—a contribution to everyone's understanding. |
| | "I suggest we…" | The psychological momentum of sharing the reply with warmth, interest and energy makes it easy to return to your agenda. |

Look back at the direction *You incline your head forward* and the commentary beside it. This sophisticated body language is part of the repertoire of leaders with strong personal authority. As long as they are acting in good faith, they are not threatened by questions and interjections, no matter how tough or emotionally loaded (example coming up).

The sharing technique works, large audience or small. I have seen many presenter trainees go from doubting to converted with a single success, then say things like, "I'm much more in control, I feel more authoritative. I don't seem to have a problem finding an answer." Most never return to the old way of locking on to the questioner.

That was the core technique. Here's the advanced application.

HANDLING FEELINGS
Accept feelings, argue facts

The toughest questions and interjections are the emotional ones, which can feel like a blow to the stomach. Yet if you're really ready to put audience needs first, you'll find even this much easier than you thought: if you're using the core technique, you are *already* handling much of the emotional charge in questions and interjections. For mild negative emotions, you're already there.

So let's make the emotions more charged.

Remember life choice 2? Choose to be comfortable with the feelings and concerns of others. That now has special meaning.

Show that you
accept the person and the feelings without judgement.
Argue only facts and logic.

That's what effective leaders do. *All* feelings, spoken and unspoken, are valid and beyond judgement. They are completely natural given that person's history up to this point. Accept the totality of the person.

The concept is too much for some.

"You must be joking. You mean if Tara Smith tells me yet again that the project is a f-----g waste of time, I'm supposed to put up with that?"

But accepting feelings is not the same thing as accepting the way they're expressed. If you get too worked up about, for example, a swearword, you can become blind to what's really happening. The feeling behind the word is far more important to you (and the audience) than the word. Take anger, for example. Hidden anger undermines you; but open anger can be exploited to increase—yes, increase—the rapport between you and your audience.

Y	"...so we're all going to have to sign the pool cars in and out."	
Q	"Oh, great!" *Sarcastic and annoyed*	
Y	*You incline your head forward, eyebrows slightly raised*	Acknowledging the feeling and the person. Here also, the interjection is a gift to you, bringing out into the open what might otherwise silently undermine your message.
	"I know. It's more bureaucracy. Nobody likes red tape, even at the best of times..."	Your words accepting and reflecting the feelings. You're not threatened by the way the feeling was expressed.
	You turn to audience.	Sharing the reply.
	"...but, we would hate the alternative a lot more. And for everyone's sake we do have to stop the system being abused.	Adding energy. Because you have accepted person and feelings, you are now free to assertively argue the facts.
	"From tomorrow morning..."	Returning to your agenda

Would you be hurt or made anxious by the sarcasm of that "Oh, great!" interjection? That's a serious issue. If you have more seniority than the interjector, you might be tempted to openly criticize the interjector's discourtesy. But that's pulling rank to compel respect, which is the best way to lose it. In the end you can't avoid a decision to replace such anxiety with the determination to look after the audience.

Better still, make a deeper decision that there is nothing to be anxious about. I like the story of the Buddhist monk who went to his abbot and complained that people in the street were mocking him by calling him a dog.

"Turn around and look at your rear end," the abbot said. "Do you see a tail wagging?"

"No," said the monk.

"Then the matter is settled," said the abbot.

Let's extend the technique. When you disagree with an interjector...

> Your manner says yes to the person and the feeling,
> even as your words say no to the person's facts.

It's got nothing to do with talking through a stiff smile, of course; an audience will see through that in a microsecond. You must truly accept the person and his feelings.

Then, most audiences will listen to you. Modern neuroscience says that humans are driven by feelings (right brain), not by logic (left brain). The research has found that we cannot make a decision without first checking in with our feelings.[6] When a presenter shows non-judgemental acceptance of us and our feelings, we immediately get another feeling: *I like this person* (right brain), which then prompts the decision: *I will listen a little longer* (left brain). Only then can we truly listen to an assertive argument—by the presenter—which opposes our own.

Y "...so restructuring of some sort is inevitable. We're going to-"

Q "Look, why don't you just come on out with it? You're going to make some of us redundant. Aren't you?"

You're listening carefully. Here's that gift again—feelings revealed rather than hidden. Hidden feelings can silently kill your message.

Y *You incline your head forward emphatically. Your upper body moves slightly, with it. Your eyebrows are raised.*
"Absolutely not. There will be no redundancies. We just don't need them when..."

Your manner is conveying *yes* to person and feeling, and *no* to the argument. Simultaneously. It's not a contradiction because feelings and facts are on different planes of communication. The same principle would operate even if the answer started, "No, it's too soon to know that yet...."

---

[6] Source, Daniel Goleman, *Emotional Intelligence*, 1995

Are you convinced by that forward inclination of the head? It may seem more logical to shake your head at that moment. And if you want to rely just on the language of logic, it is. But a good communicator is also fluent in the language of feelings and uses both simultaneously. A shake of the head can easily be taken as a blanket rejection of person, feelings and facts, which often means the audience won't believe your answer about the facts.

Many presenters find it hard to cope with such in-your-face emotion, so they enter what seems to be an escape tunnel which bears this sign: *Answer only the face value of the words, pretending that no one has any strong feelings*. In that last example such a reaction might emerge as a low-energy, flat-toned, "It's not the intention of management to make anyone redundant. Now, as I was saying…" Such a response would raise a howl of disbelief and anger. The escape tunnel turns out to lead directly into the lion enclosure.

Do you see the beauty of the technique? You can win at all levels. You convey respect, you get respected and listened to even when you assertively disagree with a faction in the audience. You can enjoy a vigorous, noisy argument with your audience without turning feelings against you. Magic.

Here's a useful device.

Sometimes check what the audience thinks or feels

Y	"So if you plant this variety a month earlier, you're likely to-"	
Q	"Look that's crap! I paid good money for that rubbish last year and I got nothing out of it."	You're surprised, but still listening with warmth and interest. Here's the gift, again.
Y	*You incline your head forward. Hearing a murmur from someone else, you turn to the audience of 50 farmers.* "Anyone else feel the same? *Scan the audience*	Checking with the audience. Adding energy. You're accepting the feelings, showing concern and interest. You want to know. Note the use of the word 'feel' rather than 'think'.
	"Two… no, three. Okay, I'd like to get to the bottom of that. Perhaps the three of you could have a word with me afterwards…	Respecting the dissenters
	All right, let's move on."	Returning to your agenda

112 How do I handle questions and interjections?

Here's a tougher test. We'll use the same example, but this time the majority feel aggressive and are not interested in anything but sorting out their quarrel with you.

Q	"Look that's crap! I paid good money for that rubbish last year and I got nothing out of it."	You're surprised, but still listening with warmth and interest. Here's another gift of audience feeling.
Y	*You incline your head forward. There's a* strong *murmur of agreement, so you turn to the audience questioningly.* "A lot of you feel the same way?"	Checking with the audience. Adding energy. Accepting the feelings.
	There's another and stronger murmur from a clear majority. Most are scowling at you, some look puzzled. One speaks.	As the extent of the problem becomes clear, you're conveying more surprise and more concern.
Q	"None of us are going to have that rubbish on again. You've got a fucking nerve trying to sell it to us."	You're **still** listening with warmth and interest—*even though they are now questioning your personal integrity.*
Y	*You incline your head forward again, then look away in silence while you think. Then you turn again to the audience.*	Acknowledging, then conveying that you're taking it very seriously.
	"Let me check something. How many of you had problems? Can you indicate with your hands...?" *At least 40 raise hands.* "Okay. How many of you took a decent yield?" *Four raise hands. A few shrug uncertainly.*	You're checking with audience, adding energy. You're keen to resolve this for the audience. Although there's a potential sales disaster looming, you're not defensive.
	"Thank you. Well, we obviously need to change course. It'll be a waste of time dealing with anything else till we sort this one out. Do you agree?"	Expert facilitation. In this case, moving on means a change in your own agenda in response to the needs of the audience. Abandoning the prepared format like this is not a

How do I handle questions and interjections?

Q *A few nods, then a murmur of assent. Many look sceptical, but some expressions show grudging respect.*	failure—it's an achievement. You're not going to win the audience on the specific problem, but you are earning their respect.
Y "Before we do that, I want to tell you most strongly that we had no idea of the problem. It did not show up in the trials.	Your chances of them accepting this declaration are now very good, because you got to grips with their feelings before stating your own.
Q *There are a few nods.*	
Y "I'm wondering about frost susceptibility. Can you give me your experience on that? Who planted early in the foothills?"	

How to handle a persistent interjector

Amy is a thorn in your side. She's worked up about forthcoming changes to the lighting in the reception area, when you're trying to tell the staff about refurbishment of the whole floor. This is the fourth time she's interrupted on the same point and she didn't take your last hint that it's time to move on.

Again, check with the audience.

Q "Listen. I want to come back to the reception lighting. I think it's important to-".	
Y *You put your hand up in the stop position.* "Just a moment, I need to check this..." *Look around questioningly.* "Is it useful for everyone if we stay with the lighting problem?"	Not using her name. You're inviting the audience to decide on a topic, not to make a judgement of Amy

Now there are two possible outcomes, both of them easily controlled. If the audience is fed up with Amy's constant interruptions, they'll shake their heads and ask to move on. In which case you won't hear from Amy again, because the psychological weight of an audience is huge. You should take care of Amy's dignity by turning back to her to suggest that you meet to talk about it afterwards. But if the audience indicates that the lighting problem is important to them, then you have the perfect excuse to give Amy more time.

How to handle audience anger when you deserve it

Even now, the same principles apply, provided that whatever mistake you made was done in good faith.

Let's suppose you're accused unexpectedly and you realize instantly that the accusation is right. Remember for this example that you must never compound a mistake by flogging yourself when you admit it. (See *How to apologize or admit a mistake* p96)

Y	"...so I've arranged for Tania, Hans, and Peter to go to the Berlin conference."	
	There's an immediate buzz. Heads turn. People look at each other in surprise and anger.	
	"A problem?"	Checking with the audience.
Q	*Accusing tone.* "I'll say. The new protocol says *all* district managers go to Santiago."	
Y	"How's that?"	
Q	"We've all re-arranged our schedules. You handed us the protocol two days ago and asked us to read it carefully."	As you hear this, you're puzzled, but not defensive.
Y	*Turn to audience.* "Anyone got a copy here?"	
	One hands a page to you and points. You read, nod, hand it back, and turn to audience.	It's a normal nod, this time. You're agreeing with the facts presented to you.
	"Right. My apologies, everyone—I set you wrong. I asked you to read it carefully, and I obviously didn't do so myself.	Regret, yes. But no humility, indignity or embarrassment. Your character is much too strong to feel threatened by any one mistake.

> "You'll need that resolved, pronto. You might like to help yourselves to coffee while I talk to head office."

With this kind of apology, you have everything to gain. Respect for you will increase. And, interestingly, the same is true for children and parents. Next time you accuse your child of breaking the vase and then discover that it was the cat, apologize without humility, indignity or embarrassment. Your child will love it and love you for it.

Which brings back a memory. Once, when I did exactly that with my youngest son, a huge, warm smile broke out on his face. He looked as if he was going to hug me; instead he raced off to tell his brother, "Hey, Andrew, Dad stuffed up!"

Loss of dignity? None. Gain in trust? Plenty.

Incidentally, an audience of children can see through you even faster than an audience of adults.

Answering closed questions

Look at this classic way to get a howl of derision from the audience.

Interjector	"Minister, when will you announce the drought assistance measures?"
Minister	"Well, this is a complex situation that will involve at least two select committees and more than likely we'll need to consult with affected parties in towns throughout the affected provinces. It's also vital, for the sake for those who have suffered most, that we don't rush this if we're going to-"
Interjector	"Minister, I think what you're trying to say is that you haven't got a clue."

Sounds deceptive and defensive, doesn't it? Most politicians and many senior executives have been infected with a virus that makes them start explaining at A so that you don't get your answer until they reach Z. Audiences can't stand it and it turns media interviewers into attack dogs: "Minister, it's a simple enough question. When will you make the announcement?"

The answer is so very simple. It's not a murder mystery. When asked a closed question (that's a question seeking a factual answer):

116 How do I handle questions and interjections?

> Put the end at the beginning—with one word or a short phrase—*then* explain or qualify as necessary.

The minister's answer may well have been perfectly genuine, but by leaving the point to the end he undermined his own credibility. The point was that he didn't know yet. All he had to do was start with: "I can't tell you yet. This is a complex..." etc. It's a mystery that so many politicians don't seem to have discovered that way to answer a question.

When the interjection doesn't need verbal attention

Many interjections are so fleeting, so lightweight, that it would be ludicrous to spend words on them. But there is one element of the technique you still need. Warmth.

Y	"So, on Thursday night, Rachel and I aim to get together to-"	
Q	"Hah!" *Light hearted.*	
Y	*You continue almost without pause, raising one eyebrow, a hint of amusement in the eyes, no more than a glance at the interjector.*	You're taking it in passing, with warm acceptance. No words are needed at all.
	"...to work out how to get everyone involved in..."	

Handling the hidden agenda

> "The most important thing in communication is to hear what isn't being said." *Peter F. Drucker*

The needles of stinging nettle are so small they're nearly invisible, but they still bring a thoroughly unpleasant result, especially when brushed lightly. In an audience, the hidden agenda (or barely-concealed emotion) is much the same. Your first instinct is often to brush it off, though the brushing simply injects more poison into your presentation.

However, take a lesson from the goat. Tiptoe through the nettle patch and you're likely to find a goat in the middle of it, not only eating the nettle, but getting a nourishing meal from it. He knows how to handle stinging nettle: grip it directly and firmly, then it doesn't hurt.

Grasp the nettle directly.

An example: you're to deliver a talk to government officials and child abuse experts on the dangers of letting a disturbed child talk to anyone who believes child-abuse is rampant. As you speak, you notice two or three expressions becoming sour. No-one makes a sound, but there are sidelong glances. Significant looks. The audience is disturbed by something you're not party to. A hidden agenda.

Do you do anything about it? Yes, you do, because your talk will fail if you don't. Hidden does not mean harmless. I've chosen an example with very strong passions to demonstrate how easy it is to handle as long as you are acting in good faith.

	You pause, and look around.	
Y	"Am I missing something?"	Checking with the audience. There are many ways to check with the audience. For example: "There's something you want to tell me?" or "Some of you don't seem happy about this." or "What's happening?"
Q	*A women delivers her words with anger.*	
	"I resent your implication that innocent men get convicted as a result of psychologists beliefs."	You're listening with warmth and interest. This interjection would normally sting, but when you welcome it as a gift, there's no sting.
	There's a buzz of support.	
Y	*You look around questioningly.*	
	"Looks like you're not the only one who feels that strongly."	Accepting and reflecting the feelings.
	A woman sitting next to her speaks without rising. If anything, she's even angrier than the first one.	

118 How do I handle questions and interjections?

Q	"Every time we've called in the police, we've got a conviction. Our methods are accurate and well proven."	
Y	"So you feel that psychologists can successfully separate themselves from their own beliefs?"	You're specifically checking and reflecting feelings. There's no need for you to be threatened at all. You are facilitating constructive exchange for the audience.
Q	"I can't speak for all psychologists, but objectivity is part of our training and methodology."	
Y	*Nod again, looking round. Some are shaking their heads.*	
	"Other opinions?"	You're inviting cross-fire.

Handling cross-fire

Your manner and body language says you are allowing the cross-fire to happen as a useful part of your presentation. It says you're still in control and may step in directly at any time. Notice that with this system, there is no need, ever, to feel insecure, as long as you are acting in good faith.

	Audience members direct comments to each other and to the audience.	
Q1	"I think he's right. It's gone too far. My husband won't stop to help a child who's fallen off her bike. He's terrified of getting accused."	You're listening to every interjection on behalf of the whole audience, even though one side is vehemently opposed to your message.
Q2	"Rubbish. It's been proven that children simply do not lie about these things!"	
Q1	"I agree they usually don't lie. But their beliefs and memories are changed unwittingly	

	by supposed experts who believe that child abuse is everywhere."	
Q3	"That is outrageous. We have the highest ethical standards and constant supervision to back it up."	
Q4	"Your standards have all the delicacy of a bull in a china shop. Your good intentions pave the path to hell. You wreck lives."	
	After a few of these exchanges you hold up a hand.	
Y	"All right. Thank you. Obviously some of us are in positions that won't change overnight. Is it useful to continue, or shall we return to the agenda?"	Checking with audience. With so much emotion in the air, you do need the audience agreement to return to the original agenda.

When there's an expert in the audience

I can see it now.

"Excuse me. I disagree with your statement that Lady Margot was discourteous to Jean Harlowe..."

Oh no, an expert. She'll know more than me.

"It was more than discourtesy: when Jean Harlowe said, 'It's a pleasure to meet you Lady Margot', she pronounced it with a 't' and Lady Margot's reply was 'No my dear, it's Margot. The 't' is silent as in Harlowe.'"

The audience laughs.

"Uh..." *What a disaster. She's probably knows the hour and the day that Harlowe and Margot sneezed. They'll all think this woman should be up here instead of me. They'll think I'm a pretender. They'll think I'm a charlatan.* "Uh... good point... Well, returning to the subject at hand..."

That kind of self-talk shows how disasters are made not by what is thrown at us, but by the way we choose to respond. Yes, it is a choice—and we could avoid the disasters by focusing on what the audience needs.

First, let's correct the self-talk.

"Excuse me. I'm afraid I must take issue with your statement that Lady Margot was discourteous to Jean Harlowe."

"Of course. Go ahead." *Maybe she can add a useful perspective.*

"It was more than discourtesy: when Jean Harlowe said, 'It's a pleasure to meet you Lady Margot', she pronounced it with a 't' and Lady Margot's reply was 'No my dear, it's Margot. The 't' is silent as in Harlowe.'"

The audience laughs and you laugh with them. *Great. What a gift.* "Thank you, I stand corrected. You seem well-informed on those two."

"I've read a lot about Lady Margot."

"Well, if I can't answer a question, I'm going to ask you. All right... Let's go on to Lady Margot's last years..."

Look back at that self-talk. The most important word was *perspective*. The audience did not come to hear facts about Lady Margot. They came to hear your perspective on Lady Margot. The difference means that it doesn't matter a jot if the interjector is a walking Wikipedia.

Adopt this attitude:
The expertise of others adds value to your presentation.

Sometimes it's worth acknowledging the presence of an expert before you begin. You might squeeze it in at the end of the introduction: "I want to show you that by speeding up the day-night cycle for battery hens, you could theoretically reach a lay rate of 24 eggs a day. But before I begin, I would like to give a special welcome to Martha Lutyens. Most of you will know that Martha has a great deal of expertise in the biological effects on humans of working in an accelerated day-night cycle. Martha, if I can't answer a question, could I lay it in front of you?"

Battery hens aside, the most important points are:

- Take pleasure in acknowledging expertise.
- Be willing to take advantage of the expertise.

I know, I haven't answered a significant worry. *If I openly acknowledge the expert, very soon everyone will want to hear from them and not me.* And I don't have an answer, because it may well become true. However, any expert crass enough to actually take over will earn themselves a lot of disrespect from the audience.

When you don't know the answer

> When you don't know, say—cheerfully—
> "I don't know".

It really is as simple as that, though it might need a follow-up. You could check with the audience. "I don't know, can anyone answer that one?" But if no-one knows, undertake to find out. And did you pick up the most important word there? Cheerfully. The point is that the audience is much more wired to your personal strength than to whether or not you know something.

When the farewelled one bites back

You're farewelling a staff member and they take the opportunity to criticize the company. It's commonplace when staff are made redundant. In the following example, accepting feelings is by far the most important component. And remember that accepting feelings does not imply acceptance of the facts being offered.

Y	"Blaine, on behalf of us all, I want to wish you the very best with whatever you tackle next."	
Q	"Is that so? Well that's a right load of hypocrisy, isn't it?. If this company wished me well they wouldn't have made me redundant, would they? I work here for 30 years and those heartless bastards in head office still think I'm a statistic. I'm the fifth one this year. How bloody short-sighted to waste all this experience and get	You're acknowledging him now and then with a small forward inclination of the head. Not agreeing with him, just listening and accepting the person and the feelings. This is no time to be

some pimple-faced teenager that costs less. There, I've said my piece."

Y "Blaine..." *Turn to audience with occasional glances to Blaine.*
"...I don't think there's anyone here who doesn't know that you're going through a rough time. None of us would find it easy... You said you'll probably have a go at market gardening and all of us here really do wish you the very best of success with that. But we also hope you'll have more time to get that sailboat out on the harbour.

"Now, let's go through to the cafe. Afternoon tea is ready."

defensive. Nor is it time to argue facts and logic.

Responding only to feelings, not facts or logic.

The process reduces tension. His intention was to express feeling and you acknowledged precisely that without getting sucked into debating the face value of the words.

Of course a really angry person may persist for longer. If so, become assertive about this not being the time and place, but your manner will still carry understanding and fundamental respect. (More on farewells on p128)

Dealing with a drunk interjector

I don't mean a pleasantly relaxed interjector. I mean an interjector so lubricated, he makes the audience wince when he calls out. In that state, he often won't even respond to the very obvious disapproval of the audience. Such people are on a different planet, so treat them as if they're exactly that far away. When they call out, don't show that you noticed them at all.

Nothing happened.

I've seen it sober up a drunk faster than a poke in the eye.

Of course there's a limit. If he's so plastered that he keeps calling out anyway, all you can do is turn with raised eyebrows to whoever can have the drunk ejected. When he's gone, smile *with* the audience and resume your speech.

Handling a heckler

I mean a heckler without a genuine, serious grievance. The heckling is for fun, or politically motivated, or both.

The easy answer is the same as for the drunk. Ignore him or her. It takes a courageous and persistent heckler to continue when you and an entire crowd cause him to vanish in the psychological sense.

But, there's a better answer. Better, because it's fun. Just make sure you have a very well-nourished sense of being bigger than the occasion, that you have a good sense of humour and that you want to give as good as you get. On all three counts, I salute John Morley, a British politician who had just finished a rousing campaign address by requesting his listeners to vote for him.

"I'd rather vote for the devil," a heckler chimed in.

"Quite so," Morely called back. "But if your friend declines to run, may I count on your support?" Spontaneous and inspired. Few hecklers would have a ready answer to that one.

We can't all be like Morely, of course. But we don't need to be. If you talk to large crowds, you can have heckler-repartee up your sleeve, ready. Here's an all-purpose example. A union official, John McKenzie, confronted with a gadfly heckler, told a ready-for-heckler story. And note that after the first two words, he shared the reply with everyone, returning to the heckler for the last three words.

"You know, (turn away from heckler to audience)... I must tell you about the farm I once lived on with my mother. She was very concerned about my behaviour back then, because I didn't have much respect for the animals. I even used to torment an old broken down donkey. 'One day,' she said to me, 'that donkey is going to come back and haunt you.' (turn back to heckler) and *here he is!"*

It wouldn't do any harm to watch out for a few one-line heckler-killers like these:

"I can see that you're not a complete idiot. Obviously some parts are missing."

"Are you sure you should be here? I mean it's a full moon out there."

"I refuse to have a battle of wits with an unarmed person."

"Truly, it's amazing to think that you beat out 50 million other sperm."

"Yes, April the first—a very significant date for my friend here."

And if you're wondering about fundamental respect, don't. The comments are so clearly outrageous and light-hearted, you don't compromise respect for the individual. Just be sure that it really is heckling, not a genuine question or grievance.

Chapter 7 How do I handle formal or special occasions?

This chapter offers a modern way to tackle formal or special occasions that our great-grandparents would recognize and their great-grandparents before them. In many special occasions, formal language is not only acceptable, it lends an expected sense of importance and audiences would feel let down without it.

But formality should never mean coldness or aloofness. Human warmth is still the magic ingredient.

Formal salutations

If you were to have a bad dream about it, it might go like this: you open your mouth to speak, but you only get as far as, "Your Worship..." when you notice that the entire audience is composed of people wearing braid, ribbon and heavy golden metal. They all have telephones in front of them, and they all have fingers poised, ready to dial lawyers should you damage their sense of importance and propriety.

Salutations never need be a problem. Solve it in advance.

- Ask the organizer whether the occasion really warrants formality. His Worship the Mayor, Sir Terence Bolton-Smythe might not thank you for singling him out for formal salutation as you launch into the nineteenth hole pep talk.

- Ask the organizer for the correct salutations and order.

- Check the pronunciation of unfamiliar names.

- Don't allow formality to dehumanise your salutations. Under all their titles, letters and braid, they are also real people who need the same warmth you would have for anyone you just met in the corridor. Say Your Worship, Sir Thomas, Doctor Jones, Councillor Talbot, Mr Fulton, with pleasure in your eyes and tone. They will be pleasantly surprised, because they have heard far too many flat-toned, empty, ritualized salutations and greetings.

Introducing a speaker

The audience needs you to put perspective on what they're about to hear and who they're about to hear it from.

- Introduce the topic, explaining its importance to the audience.
- Introduce the speaker, explaining that person's connection to the topic. Give the speaker's qualifications or experience, but also give a *personal* introduction. You may need to ask around to find a personal, illustrative anecdote

"Good morning everyone. As you all know, the recent rudder-control failure has put the whole industry under a cloud and endangered the reputations we have all built up. I think you'd agree that the best protection we have is to increase our efforts to learn more and make sure it never happens again.	Introducing the topic. Explaining its importance to the audience.
"I'd like to introduce you to Sybil Schreiber from Seattle. I'm sure you've heard about her international reputation in hydraulic control systems. But you may not know that Sybil was once a stunt flier. Her party trick was to stand on the wing of a Pitt Special, controlling ailerons and rudder with extension wires.	Introducing the speaker. Explaining the connection to the topic. Speaker's qualifications. Plus a *personal* insight.
You'll be glad to hear that her safety skills have developed beyond number 8 fencing wire. Please welcome Sybil Schreiber."	

Don't upstage, gazump or oversell the speaker

When you introduce a speaker, it's a mistake to try to impress the audience with your own performance abilities. That's upstaging and extremely discourteous. If in doubt, tone your performance down while keeping your natural warmth.

Gazumping means giving the speech the speaker is about to give. It can be very tempting if you get into your enthusiastic stride and it has led to some caustic comments by speakers about how little there is left to say.

Also, in your enthusiasm, don't oversell the speaker. "And I'd like you to welcome Jimmy Jones who is the most thrilling speaker in Britain today and I'm sure he's going to make our eyeballs pop with the most exciting talk of our lives." Say that and Jimmy Jones has too much to live up to. He'll go home afterwards and stick pins in a wax dummy that looks like you.

Thanking a speaker

The audience needs you to put an audience-centred perspective on what they've just heard and (sometimes) on the person they've heard it from. Notice that with the method below, there is no need to praise a speaker for giving a good speech when it wasn't.

- During the speaker's talk, listen for something that moves the audience's feelings; interest or insight, surprise, delight, shock, horror, and so on. No matter how bad the speech itself, there is always something.

- When you speak, re-visit the specific part you picked out. You may want to own those feelings personally, but you'll also need to imply audience involvement.

- Move from specific to general, reflecting the new perspective.

- Finally, thank the speaker.

"Rolf, I was delighted to hear that it's now possible to save trees that have been almost completely ring barked. I'm sure no-one here missed the significance for native saplings in deer country.	Revisiting something that involved audience feelings.
Your talk has given us new insight into the science of native bush management generally. A most valuable session, and I'm	Moving from specific to general.
sure everyone here will join me in expressing our thanks."	Thanking the speaker.

The process works even if the audience disagrees with the whole speech. You can always find something that added perspective, and therefore value. When the audience and you are opposed to everything said, you can still truthfully say, "Dougal, as you've obviously noticed, many of us don't accept your argument. But I think those of us who argued the most would be the first to appreciate the fact that you have helped us understand your point of view. So on behalf..."

Again, be careful of upstaging. And don't over-thank for a poor performance; effusive praise for what the speaker knows was barely passable will be acutely embarrassing for everyone.

Farewelling a staff member or colleague

> "When a man retires and time is no longer a matter of urgent importance, his colleagues generally present him with a watch." *R.C. Sheriff.*

Here's a classic mistake.

The CEO farewells employee, Simon Smith, who is thoroughly disliked. So he gives Simon a farewell that is grudging and insulting by omission. The smile is a mask, the good wishes breathtakingly short. Everyone knows that Simon is being damned with a faint-hearted farewell. But to the CEO's amazement, his farewell of this unpopular character is badly received by the staff. He's not getting the warm vibes he thought he would get. How could that be?

Saints are not over-represented in the population. Few earn unrestrained accolades when they leave the company. So when the audience watches you farewell one of their colleagues, part of each person is thinking, *I wonder how I'll get farewelled when I leave.*

Also, the audience is aware of another dimension. They are part of an organization which is saying good-bye to part of itself. Much though they dislike Simon, as an audience they want him farewelled with fundamental respect. A manager who ignores that invites trouble. At a farewell, your leadership qualities are being weighed and balanced in a way you won't find at any other occasion.

You don't have to lie.

With fundamental respect you can gracefully farewell anyone without taking liberties with the truth. You can refer to disagreements, even blazing rows, with no loss of respect, though of course such references mustn't be lengthy. Your 'self-talk' as you speak in front of the person should be like this: *I want to give you the best and most dignified farewell possible. By doing so, I don't just honour you, I honour everyone in this room including myself.*

- Research by finding an incident or story about the person leaving that shows a positive insight on their character. There's always something. You may have to research their private life through friends to find something suitable, though friends are usually more than willing. Use that incident to give a personal, constructive insight on the person leaving.

- If there are major negative feelings associated with the person *and* if the audience is aware of them, refer to them in a non-judgmental way. "As you know, Henry and I haven't seen eye-to-eye on every issue... (allow for a wry smile, perhaps a restrained laugh from the audience) even so, I have valued the way he..." Such openness is important, so that no-one goes away referring to you as a hogwash-pusher.

- Outline the history of that person in your organization, highlighting achievement. If appropriate, talk about the constructive influence that person has had on your organization. Tell illustrative anecdotes.

- Tell the audience something of his or her future plans.

- Make the presentation, wish him or her well for the future and invite applause.

When you know the person well, it can be tempting to run a joke or two at his expense. But beware, a joke that would have him and everyone else rolling in the aisles around a canteen table won't always work at a farewell. If you're in doubt, ask yourself if the joke diminishes that person's stature with this audience. If it does, the joke will also diminish your own stature in the eyes of the very people who laugh at your wit.

Have fun, make it a warm-hearted occasion, but don't forget that feelings like sadness and anxiety are often lurking under the surface. Dignity and respect are just about everything at a farewell.

When the farewelled one bites back
See p121

When it's you being farewelled.

- Thank the person expressing the farewell.
- EITHER: Express gratitude to the company and any relevant individuals. Say what being with the company has meant to you. (That could be described as the 'correct form'.)

  OR: Speak your mind about the company, expressing feelings in a controlled manner. Be seen to be bigger than your own feelings and in command of them. Even if your feelings are negative, still convey warmth to individuals present. If that's too hard, don't leave out the fundamental respect which should survive all differences.

- Say what you're going to do with the gift.
- Say what your plans are. Or, if they've been mentioned already, add some personal insight to them. Make people smile. It's their last feeling about you before you leave.

Presenting and receiving awards

The presentation speech

- Tell an anecdote that makes a point about the recipient's qualities.
- Relate those qualities to the award or presentation. The origin of the award may be relevant. Very often the person who established it did want to recognize particular qualities in a recipient.
- Outline what the recipient did to earn the award.
- Present the award.

Receiving an award

"Ladies and gentlemen, I feel overwhelmed and humble to be standing here before you..."

Oh dear, oh dear. How many times have we heard that? If it's not obviously heartfelt, it comes across as a yawn-maker. The most effective acceptance speech I have ever seen was that of the young New Zealander, Anna Paquin, receiving her Oscar in '94. When she opened her mouth to speak, nothing came out but strangled gasps. Now she *was* overwhelmed, and so obviously genuine that she endeared herself to millions.

If you're not so affected, try this.

- Thank the person who presented it to you. If appropriate, thank the organizers.

- Give the audience an insight into what motivated you.

- Tell them what you'll do with the award. Paint a picture, perhaps say where you're going to place it: on the mantel-piece etc.

- Tell them what's next for you. For example, if you've won a road race, you might tell them that you don't intend to touch your running shoes again for three weeks. It'll take that long to get them through the de-contamination unit.

Opening functions

- Thank whoever introduced you.

- Give your reasons for wanting to be here. It's not enough to vaguely suggest that everything will be interesting; find something specific about the function that you find interesting and say so.

- Tell the audience the significance of the function. Tell them who will benefit from it.

- Thank the organizers.

- Officially declare the function open.

Funerals

In British-derived cultures, there have been countless funerals where the departing spirit must have looked in amazement at the rigidly brave faces, listened with incredulity to the glowing tributes and said, "I must be at the wrong funeral." On the earthly side of the veil, the combination of stiff upper lip and false tribute has wrought lasting psychological damage on loved ones who never got to grips with one of the main reasons for a funeral. It's a chance to grieve openly with community support.

Fortunately for collective sanity, that's changing. A funeral is the place for tears and weeping and other expression of feelings, including joy and celebration of life.

Here's a funeral that stood out as an excellent farewell. An eight-year-old boy died in an accident. He was a well-known lad with a normal boyish mixture of charm and mischief. The funeral service was held at his school. His desk was brought outside for the service, complete with books and chair, and the children filed past his open coffin, many of them weeping. The speeches were a mix of emotions. His brother said, "He was a pest sometimes but I loved him anyway." His sister shouted at him directly, "Daniel, I'm really angry with you for going. I just wanted you to know that." His father cried, his mother read from Kahlil Gibran. "Your children are not your children. They are the sons and daughters of Life's longing for itself." Then, every child in Daniel's class released lighter-than-air balloons so that he could have company getting to heaven.

- *Sometimes speak directly to the departed.* Even if you don't believe in life after death, you're speaking to the part of the deceased that lives vividly in the minds of the audience in front of you. You'll be honouring them and their memory of their loved one.

- *Tell stories.* Find anecdotes that illustrate a point. Use gentle humour, sometimes directly to departed. "Pierre, do you remember that time you got us thrown out of the Sistine Chapel? You'd smuggled in a loaf of bread but the crumbs kept dropping out and the pigeons followed you in. Well, I hope you've been more successful this time."

- *Express your own feelings directly.* Not, "Janine was good with children.", but, "I love the way Janine had with children." Or better still, "Janine, I really loved the way children wanted to be with you and play with you." Feelings are the best truth. Even raw or crudely expressed, they are worth more than carefully constructed phrases, elaborate ritual or expensive caskets. Imagine this, said in tears, "I wish you were still here to clean me out at poker, you old bastard!"

- *Express negative feelings as well as the positive.* If it's negative, don't dwell on historical detail, just express your feelings. "Stephen, I was angry with you for years. Then I wanted to go back to being friends, but I never got a chance to tell you until now. Well, I could have made a chance, but it was hard to do. I'm really sorry. Now I want to say that..."

There's more dignity in honesty than in a whitewash. If you're going to pretend that you always liked the person or that they suddenly assumed a halo when he or she died, you might as well change their name when you refer to them. If you have an emotional debt to the departed then a whitewash covers over your own dry rot which will continue to eat away at you.

Sometimes refer to the human frailties of the deceased. Not that you should trot out a whole list; refer to them sparingly in a way that strengthens fundamental respect.

- *Don't fight the tears.* Allow them to happen, even while speaking, even if they make you stop and start. Tears are the noble language of the eye—the greatest honour you can give the departed and everyone present.

Other family and friends speeches

Weddings, twenty-firsts, anniversaries, birthdays, re-unions, success celebrations, and many more can easily be dealt with using the city-model preparation method. But, there are some refinements you may find useful.

Formality and informality

If you live in an egalitarian society, this can be a difficult one. Many people believe that a family 'do' is one occasion when you can throw formality out the window, but the same people often find themselves better satisfied by a little formal pizzazz. As we saw earlier, formality lends importance. If you reject it out of hand, you may be depriving the family stars of some of the special feeling that should go with the function. A formality like "I call on you to charge your glasses to toast the young couple" may mean a very special moment for that couple, even though the same couple express little respect for traditional values.

Whatever you decide, never mistake the formal trappings for the heart of the message.

Formalities are the fanfare, not the message.

In other words, once you've uttered the formal words, go back to talking informally, to real people, to make your message.

(Taps glass) "Good evening everyone. Tonight, it's my pleasant task to propose the toast to Mum and Dad as they leave for Patagonia.	A formal flourish to lend importance to the occasion.
Pause, smile	Flagging the shift to informality.
"Mum, I can't resist this, I'm going to tell everyone what you said fifteen years ago when..-"	Now talking in simple, informal, direct, personal language.
"Oh no... you remembered!"	
(To Mum) "I certainly did.	
(To audience) "When I was heading off to the Andes, you know what Mum said to me? She said, 'Are you out of your mind?' (laughter) So on behalf of everyone here I want to wish a couple of fine people a wonderful trip even though they are obviously already out to lunch. Mum and Dad."	

Tell stories, anecdotes

They work well in any speech, but for family and friends, stories and anecdotes are priceless.

Here's a suggestion if you have young children. Get a sturdy notebook and record the funny things they do and say, recording the date they happened. In my family, that notebook has become a prized source of laughter as our boys read glimpses of their past. They're so proud of the notebook, they show their friends. When Sam gets married, I'm going to publicly warn the bride about the day he wiped out a dishwasher, a window and a briefcase, and broke a hammer on the piano. When discovered, he ticked *us* off. He wagged his finger at us and said, "You don't shout at me, you don't send me to sit on the stairs, I go sit on the stairs myself."

But don't just tell a story and leave it at that.

- Tell the story

- Give it a point.

"I'll always remember the time Annette waded into a crowd of young hoods who were tormenting a chap with Down's Syndrome. Stood right in the middle of them with her arm round the victim, cutting them to ribbons with her tongue. Half their size, she was. They just stood there with their mouths open.	Telling the story.
"That was courage. I was so proud of her. And I'm proud of Annette now and not a bit surprised to see her taking on a challenge like this..."	Giving it a point.

OR

"Tomàs, I hope you weren't expecting a peaceful life with my daughter...	Making the point in advance.
"I'm warning you now, when you have a shower, *lock the door.* Once, she burst in on me washing my hair in the shower and asked at the top of her voice, 'What means God?' I put my head out of the water with the brilliant reply, 'What?' And she said, 'If God doesn't get food does he die?' So I said, 'Can this wait?' So then..."	Telling the story.

But is *it funny?*

Family gatherings can be excruciatingly painful if the speaker gets the jokes wrong. Time and again I've seen good atmospheres soured, with smiles becoming more and more frozen as the so-called funny stories go on. Some speakers hear laughter—even embarrassed laughter—and take it as approval to continue along the same horrible path.

The test is the same as for farewells. If the story is going to make them look human, fine. If it's going to make them look small, leave it out.

Expressions of affection

It's so easy to be carried away with the process of giving an entertaining and interesting message that you can forget the most important message of all. Ideally, family occasions are an expression of love more than a matter of duty. In some way, your message has to convey that. Many people find direct expressions of affection or love difficult even in private and within a nuclear family. Families are the poorer for it.

The same goes for many social gatherings, where an expression of affection has potential for enriching everyone present.

If you live in a family that's uneasy with open displays of feeling, here's a way you can do so with reasonable ease at a family and friends gathering: start with a touch of formality. I've seen it done well by a friend at his father's eightieth birthday.

He tapped his glass with a spoon. "Excuse me everyone. I want to propose a toast to Dad. Dad, we're not a demonstrative family, I know. We don't usually tell each other our feelings about anything. But I think this is one time when it's right for us to tell you that we love you... and that we hope your *ninetieth* birthday will be even better than this one."

Selected quotable quotes

Next to being witty yourself, the best thing is being able to quote another's wit. *Christian N. Bovee.*

This selection is entirely personal; they either move me or make me laugh. My apologies to the prolific genius known as *Anon.*

accomplish
I long to accomplish a great and noble task, but it is my chief duty to accomplish small tasks as if they were great and noble. *Helen Keller*

adultery
Do infants enjoy infancy as much as adults enjoy adultery? *Anon*

adversity
Adversity has the effect of eliciting talents which in prosperous circumstances would have lain dormant. *Horace*

I'll say this for adversity: people seem to be able to stand it, and that's more than I can say for prosperity. *Kin Hubbard*

advertising
Advertising may be described as the science of arresting the human intelligence long enough to get money from it. *Stephen Leacock*

Consumers are like roaches. You spray 'em and you spray 'em and they become immune after a while. *Marketing guru David Lubars*

advice
Advice is what we ask for when we already know the answer but wish we didn't. *Erica Jong*

age and youth
When your friends begin to flatter you on how young you look, it's a sure sign you're getting old. *Mark Twain*

Youth is wasted on the young. *George Bernard Shaw*

Inside every old person is a young person wondering what happened. *Terry Pratchett*

First you forget names, then you forget faces, then you forget to pull your zipper up, then you forget to pull it down. *Leo Rosenburg*

ambition
Most people would succeed in small things if they were not troubled by great ambitions. *Longfellow*

Most people aim at nothing in life… and hit it with amazing accuracy. *Anon*

anger
Never get angry. Never make a threat. Reason with people. *Don Corleone, The Godfather*

attitude
The great discovery of my generation is that a human being can alter his life by altering his attitudes. *William James*

Nothing in life is so hard that you can't make it easier by the way you take it. *Ellen Glasgow*

It isn't what happens to you as much as how you look at what happens to you. *Carmen dell'Orifice*

We are one hundred per cent responsible for how we experience our experience. *Marianne Williamson*

Experience is not what happens to a man; it is what a man does with what happens to him. *Aldous Huxley*

Life is like a tennis game. I can't choose how the ball is hit at me, but I can choose how I hit it back. *Margaret Moth*

autobiography
A man's face is his autobiography. A woman's face is her work of fiction. *Oscar Wilde*

An autobiography is an unrivalled vehicle for telling the truth about other people. *Philip Guedalla*

belief
Drugs are not always necessary, belief in recovery always is. *Norman Cousins*

Under all that we think, lives all we believe, like the ultimate veil of our spirits. *Antonio Machado*

The most unhappy of all men is he who believes himself to be so. *Hume.*

change
Things do not change. We change. *Henry Thoreau.*

Be the change you want to see in the world. *Mahatma Ghandi*

character
Be more concerned with your character than your reputation, because your character is what you really are, while your reputation is merely what others think you are. *John Wooden*

children
Your children are not your children. They are the sons and daughters of Life's longing for itself. *Kahlil Gibran*

A child can ask a thousand questions that the wisest man cannot answer. *J. Abbott*

church
Most of us spend the first six days of each week sowing wild oats, then we go to church on Sunday and pray for a crop failure. *Fred Allen*

commit
The moment one definitely commits oneself, then Providence moves too. *Goethe*

common sense
Common sense is the collection of prejudices acquired by age eighteen. *Albert Einstein.*

communication
The most important thing in communication is to hear what isn't being said. *Peter F. Drucker*

compassion
We have all sufficient strength to endure the misfortunes of others. *La Rochefoucauld*

confidence
A man who has confidence in himself gains the confidence of others. *Hasidic saying*

condoms
Should be used on every conceivable occasion. *Anon*

If only Mr and Mrs Hitler had used one. *Anon*

conceit
He was like a cock who thought the sun had risen to hear him crow. *George Eliot*

condemn
They condemn what they do not understand. *Cicero*

conferences
No grand idea was ever born in a conference, but a lot of foolish ideas have died there. *F. Scott Fitzgerald*

connections
All things are connected... Man did not weave the web of life, he is merely a strand in it. Whatever he does to the web, he does to himself. *Chief Seattle.*

I am a part of all that I have met. *Tennyson*

Every action in our lives touches on some chard that will vibrate in eternity. *Edwin Hubbel Chapin*

courage
At the bottom of a good deal of bravery that appears in the world there lurks a miserable cowardice. Men will face powder and steel because they cannot face public opinion. *E.H.Chapin*

creating
The world is what we think it is. If we can change our thoughts, we can change the world. *H.M.Tomlinson*

We don't see things as they are. We see things as we are. *Anais Nin*

criticism
Critics are like eunuchs in a harem: they know how it's done, they've seen it done every day, but they're unable to do it themselves. *Brendan Behan*

How do I feel about critics? How does a lamppost feel about a dog? *Anon*

cruel
The music business is a cruel and shallow money trench, a long plastic hallway where thieves and pimps run free, and good men die like dogs. There's also a negative side. *Hunter S Thompson*

death
Cowards die many times before their deaths; the valiant never taste of death but once. *Shakespeare.*

When death, the great reconciler, has come, it is never our tenderness that we repent of, but our severity. *George Eliot*

Why fear death? It is the most beautiful adventure in life. *Charles Frohman*

I'm not afraid to die, I just don't want to be there when it happens. *Woody Allen*

deathbed last words
Either this wallpaper goes, or I do. *Oscar Wilde*

defeat
What is defeat? Nothing but education, nothing but the first step to something better. *Wendell Phillips*

democracy
We go by the majority vote, and if the majority are insane, the sane must go to hospital. *H. Mann*

desires
Ours is a world where people don't know what they want and are willing to go through hell to get it. *Don Marquis*

There are two tragedies in life. One is not to get your heart's desire. The other is to get it. *George Bernard Shaw.*

destiny
I always wanted to be somebody. I see now that I should have been more specific. *Lily Tomlin*

It is not in the stars to hold our destiny, but in ourselves. *William Shakespeare*

determination
We will either find a way, or make one. *Hannibal*

If at first you don't succeed, try, try again. Then quit. There's no use being a damn fool about it. *W.C. Fields*

diet
I went on a diet, swore off drinking and heavy eating, and in 14 days I lost two weeks. *Joe Lewis*

different
It is always the minorities that hold the key of progress; it is always through those who are unafraid to be different that advance comes to human society. *Raymond B. Fosdick*

diplomacy
The art of saying "nice doggy" while you look for a stick. *Unknown*

disapproval
Lady Astor: "Mr Churchill, you're disgusting. If you were my husband, I'd poison your coffee." *Churchill*: "Madam, if you were my wife, I'd drink it."

discontent
Discontent is the first step in the progress of a man or a nation. *Oscar Wilde*

dog
We had to have the dog put down for worrying sheep. It used to slink up to them and whisper, 'Mint sauce'. *Public Speaker's Treasure Chest*

drink
Lady Astor: "Mr Churchill, you're drunk." *Churchill*: "Yes, madam, but you're ugly and in the morning I'll be sober."

Work is the curse of the drinking class. *Oscar Wilde*

duty
When a stupid man is doing something he is ashamed of, he always declares that it is his duty. *George Bernard Shaw*

emotion
There can be no transforming of darkness into light and of apathy into movement without emotion. *Carl Jung*

enemies
Always forgive your enemies. Nothing annoys them so much. *Oscar Wilde*

The greatest happiness is to vanquish your enemies, to chase them before you, to rob them of their wealth, to see those dear to them bathed in tears, to clasp to your bosom their wives and daughters. *Genghis Khan*

environment
When the insects take over the world we hope they will remember, with gratitude, how we took them along on all our picnics. *Bill Vaughn*

existence
The visible world is the invisible organization of energy. *Physicist Heinz Pagels*

facts
I don't care much for facts, am not much interested in them. You can't stand a fact up, you've got to prop it up, and when you move to one side a little and look at it from that angle, it's not thick enough to cast a shadow in that direction. *William Faulkner*

failure
What would you attempt to do if you knew you couldn't fail? *Robert Schiller*

family
He's a good boy. Everything he steals he brings right home to his mother. *Fred Allen*

Parents are the last people on earth who ought to have children. *Samuel Butler*

The first half of our life is ruined by our parents and the second half by our children. *Clarence Darrow*

We learn from experience. A man never wakes up his second baby just to see it smile. *Grace Williams*

famous last words
Heavier-than-air flying machines are impossible. *Lord Kelvin, President, Royal Society 1895*

Everything that can be invented has been invented. *Charles Duell, Commissioner U.S. Office of patents 1899*

This 'telephone' has too many shortcomings to be seriously considered as a means of communication. The device is inherently of no value to us. *Western Union internal memo 1876*

I think there is a world market for maybe five computers. *Thomas Watson, Chairman, IBM, 1943*

Airplanes are interesting toys but of no military value. *Marshal Foch, Professor of Strategy, School of War*

Computer games don't affect kids; I mean if Pac-man affected us as kids, we'd all be running around in darkened rooms, munching magic pills and listening to repetitive electronic music. *Kristian Wilson, Nintendo, Inc. 1989*

fashion
Fashion is a form of ugliness so intolerable it has to be altered every six months. *Anon*

faults
Men do not suspect faults which they do not commit. *Samuel Johnson*

fear
Do the thing you're afraid to do and the death of fear is certain. *Ralph Waldo Emerson*

flabbergasted
Defn: appalled by how much weight you've gained.

flatulence
Defn: the emergency vehicle that picks you up after you've been run over by a steamroller.

forgiveness
To forgive is to set a prisoner free, and to know that the prisoner was me. *Anon*

fortune
Fortune is not on the side of the faint-hearted. *Sophocles*

freedom
Liberty means responsibility. That is why most men dread it. *George Bernard Shaw*

While there is a lower class I am in it; while there is a criminal element I am of it; while there is a soul in prison, I am not free. *Eugene Victor Debs*

future
The trouble with our times is that the future isn't what it used to be. *Paul Valery*

genius
There is no great genius without tincture of madness. *Seneca*

gentleness
The greatest strength is gentleness. *Iroquois saying*

giving and receiving
He who waits to do a great deal of good at once, will never do anything. *Samuel Johnson*

And there are those who give and know not pain in giving, nor do they seek joy, nor give with mindfulness of virtue; They give as in yonder valley the myrtle breathes its fragrance into space. *Kahlil Gibran*

Rich gifts wax poor when givers prove unkind. *William Shakespeare*

God
I sometimes think that God in creating man somewhat over-estimated His ability. *Oscar Wilde*

God will forgive me; that's His business. *Public Speaker's Treasure Chest*

If only God would give me some clear sign! Like making a large deposit in my name at a Swiss bank. *Woody Allen*

good advice
I always pass on good advice. It's the only thing to do with it. It's never any use to oneself. *Oscar Wilde*

good and bad
There is nothing either good or bad, but thinking makes it so. *Shakespeare.*

Of the good in you I can speak, but not of the evil. For what is evil but good tortured by its own hunger and thirst. *Kahlil Gibran*

government
The best government is a benevolent tyranny tempered by an occasional assassination. *Voltaire*

There's no trick to being a humorist when you have the whole government working for you. *Will Rogers*

great
The great man is he that does not lose his child's-heart. *Mencius*

hangover
The wrath of grapes.

happiness
Happiness in intelligent people is the rarest thing I know. *Ernest Hemingway*

Happiness is good health and a bad memory. *Ingrid Bergman*

If only we'd stop trying to be happy we'd have a pretty good time. *Edith Wharton*

hatred and fear
You've got to be taught to be afraid, of people who's eyes are oddly made, and people who's skin is a diff'rent shade. You've got to be carefully taught. You've got to be taught before it's too late, before you are six or seven or eight. To hate all the people your relatives hate, you've got to be carefully taught. *Lyrics from the musical South Pacific*

heaven
In heaven, all the interesting people are missing. *Friedrich Nietzsche*

Ah, but a man's reach should exceed his grasp, or what's a heaven for? *Robert Browning*

heredity
Help! I'm being held prisoner by my heredity and environment! *Dennis Allen.*

honour
The louder he talked of his honour, the faster we counted our spoons. *Ralph Waldo Emerson*

When faith is lost and honour dies, the man is dead. *John G. Whittier*

idealist
An idealist is a man with both feet planted firmly in the air. *Franklin D. Roosevelt*

imagination
We are what and where we are because we have first imagined it. *Donald Curtis*

Willpower is much less effective than imagination. *Wayne W. Dyer*

Imagination is more important than knowledge. *Albert Einstein*

Imagination is reality about to be born. *Edvard Munch*

Imagination rules the world. *Napoleon Bonaparte*

Imagination is intelligence with an erection. *Victor Hugo*

immortality
Millions long for immortality who do not know what to do with themselves on a rainy Sunday afternoon. *Susan Ertz*

The only thing wrong with immortality is that it tends to go on forever. *Herb Caen*

inferior
No one can make you feel inferior without your consent. *Eleanor Roosevelt*

The woods would be very silent if no birds sang except those that sang best. *Henry Van Dyke*

intellectuals
An intellectual is a person educated beyond his intelligence. *Brandon Matthews*

integrity
Integrity needs no rules. *Albert Camus*

Inspiring
Every once in a while you come across something so inspiring and uplifting that it feels like coming home and taking off at the same time. *Ivo Soeters*

journalists
One of the most destructive forces in society is the journalist who believes that the whole world is either corrupt or incompetent and that it only remains to dig out the evidence. *Media Associates*

joy and sorrow
The deeper that sorrow carves into your being, the more joy you can contain. Is not the cup that holds your wine the very cup that was burned in the potter's oven? And is not the lute that soothes your spirit the very wood that was hollowed with knives? *Kahlil Gibran*

justice
If England treats her criminals the way she has treated me, she doesn't deserve to have any. *Oscar Wilde*

laws
Laws are spider webs through which the big flies pass and the little ones get caught. *Honoré de Balzac*

life and society
Live as if you were to die tomorrow. Learn as if you were to live forever. *Mahatma Gandhi*

All speech, action, and behaviour are fluctuations of consciousness. All life emerges from and is sustained in consciousness. The whole universe is the expression of consciousness. The reality of the universe is one unbounded ocean of consciousness in motion. *Maharishi Mahesh Yogi*

When your life is filled with the desire to see the holiness in everyday life, something magical happens: ordinary life becomes extraordinary, and the very process of life begins to nourish your soul. *Rabbi Harold Kushner*

Anybody who goes to see a psychiatrist ought to have his head examined. *Samuel Goldwyn*

May you live all the days of your life. *Jonathon Swift*

Don't take life so seriously. You're not going to get out alive anyway. *Unknown*

There is more to life than increasing its speed. *Mahatma Ghandi*

light
Due to technical difficulties the light at the end of the tunnel has been switched off. *Unknown*

limb
Why not go out on a limb. That's where the fruit is. *Mark Twain*

listening
Know how to listen and you will profit even from those who talk badly. *Plutarch*

live
Man is born to live, not to prepare to live. *Boris Pasternak*

logic
Any proposition arrived at by purely logical means is devoid of reality. *Albert Einstein*

loyalty
It goes far toward making a man faithful to let him understand that you think him so; and he that does but suspect I will deceive him, gives me a sort of right to do it. *Seneca*

love
'Tis better to have loved and lost than never to have loved at all. *Tennyson*

Your task is not to seek for love, but merely to seek and find all the barriers within yourself that you have built against it. *Rumi*

Spread love everywhere you go: first of all in your own house... let no one every come to you without leaving better and happier. *Mother Teresa*

To love oneself is the beginning of a life-long romance. *Oscar Wilde*

He gave her a look you could have poured on a waffle. *Rilg Lardner*

Never go to bed mad. Stay up and fight. *Phyllis Diller*

mañana
Never put off till tomorrow what you can do the day after tomorrow. *Mark Twain*

marriage
Sing and dance together and be joyous, but let each one of you be alone, even as the strings of a lute are alone though they quiver with the same music. *Kahlil Gibran*

I have a parrot that swears, a stove that smokes and a cat that stays out at night. What would I want with a husband. *Old Yankee spinster*

medium
The medium is the message. *Marshall McLuhan*

mind
All that we are is the result of what we have thought. The mind is everything. What we think, we become. *Buddha*

A man is what he thinks all day long. *Ralph Waldo Emerson* (American philosopher 19th C)

As the fletcher whittles and makes straight his arrows, so the master directs his straying thoughts. *Buddha*

The mind is a place in itself. It can create a heaven out of hell, or a hell out of heaven. *Milton*

It is the mind that maketh good of ill, that maketh wretch or happy, rich or poor. *Edmund Spenser*

It is only liquid currents of thought that move men and the world. *Wendel Phillips*

miracle
There are two ways to live your life. One is as though nothing is a miracle. The other is as though everything is a miracle. *Albert Einstein*

A miracle cannot prove what is impossible; it is useful only to confirm what is possible. *Maimonides*

mirror
A loving person lives in a loving world. A hostile person lives in a hostile world. Everyone you meet is your mirror. *Ken Keyes, Jr*

Everything that irritates us about others can lead us to an understanding of ourselves. *Carl Gustav Jung*

We cannot change anything unless we accept it. *Carl Gustav Jung*

misers
Misers aren't fun to live with, but they make wonderful ancestors. *Dave Brenner*

mission
Here is a test to find whether your mission on Earth is finished: If you're alive, it isn't. *Richard Bach*

mistakes
A man who makes no mistakes does not usually make anything. *Edward J. Phelps*

motivation
Every production of genius must be the production of enthusiasm. *Benjamin Disraeli*

A nation is a society united by a delusion about its ancestry and by a common hatred of its neighbours. *Dean William R. Inge*

morals
Moral indignation is jealousy with a halo on. *H G Wells*

nature
Nature is the living, visible garment of God. *Goethe*

Nature is the most thrifty thing in the world; she undergoes change, but there's no annihilation—the essence remains. *T. Binney*

negligent
Defn: a condition in which you absentmindedly answer the door in your nightie.

noble
It is more noble to give yourself completely to one individual than to labour diligently for the salvation of the masses. *Dag Hammarskjold*

nonsense
No one is exempt from talking nonsense; the misfortune is to do it solemnly. *Montaigne*

now
The present extends forever. It is so beautiful and so clean and free of guilt that nothing but happiness is there. *A Course for Miracles*

pain
Much of your pain is self-chosen. It is the bitter potion by which the physician within you heals your sick self. *Kahlil Gibran*

If you are distressed by anything external, the pain is not due to the thing itself, but to your own estimate of it; and this you have the power to revoke at any moment. *Marcus Aurelius*

patience
Infinite patience produces immediate results. *Unknown*

patriotism
Patriotism is the last refuge of a scoundrel. *Samuel Johnson*

A real patriot is the fellow who gets a parking ticket and rejoices that the system works. *Bill Vaughn*

people
People are not born bastards, they have to work at it. *Frank Dane*

personal abuse
She had the sort of face that always wants to see the manager. *Anon*

I refuse to have a battle of wits with an unarmed person. *Unknown*

I am not a complete idiot. Some parts are missing. *Unknown*

He used to think he was indecisive, but now he's not so sure. *Anon*

Amazing to think that you beat out 50 million other sperm. *Unknown*

I'm afraid [person] can't be here today. It was a full moon last night. *Public Speaker's Treasure Chest*

This man is depriving a village somewhere of an idiot. *Unknown*

Since he started to wear a pace-maker, every time he makes love his garage door opens. *Public Speaker's Treasure Chest*

She's descended from a long line her mother listened to. *Gypsy Rose Lee*

physics and quantum mechanics
Mind and intelligence are woven into the fabric of our universe in a way that altogether surpasses our understanding. *Freeman Dyson*

If quantum mechanics hasn't profoundly shocked you, you haven't understood it yet. *Neils Bohr and M. Kafatos*

There is no reality in the absence of observation. *Copenhagen Interpretation of Quantum Mechanics*

politics
I don't approve of political jokes, I've seen too many of them get elected. *Unknown*

He knows nothing and thinks he knows everything. That points clearly to a political career. *George Bernard Shaw*

posterity
I would much rather that posterity should inquire why no statues were erected to me, than why they were. *Cato*

press
Newspaper editors are men who separate the wheat from the chaff, then print the chaff. *Adlai Stevenson*

principles
There comes a time to put aside principles and do what's right. *Public Speaker's Treasure Chest*

When a man says he approves of something in principle, it means he hasn't the slightest intention of putting it into practice. *Prince Otto von Bismark*

public speaking
The human brain starts working the moment you are born and never stops until you stand up to speak in public. *George Jessel*

You have noticed that the less I know about a subject, the more confidence I have; and the more light I throw on it. *Mark Twain*

(After a mistake) I'd commit suicide, but then what would I do for an encore. *Toastmasters Treasure Chest*

purpose
If you don't know where you're going, any road will take you there. *Koran*

reality
Change the way you look at things and the things you look at will change. *Wayne W Dyer*

A man's life is what his thoughts make of it. *Marcus Aurelius* (Roman philosopher & sage)

rectitude
Defn: the formal dignified demeanor assumed by a procticologist immediately before he examines you.

religion
Religion is excellent stuff for keeping common people quiet. *Napoleon Bonaparte*

Men never do evil so completely and cheerfully as when they do it from religious conviction. *Blaise Pascal*

regrets
Wouldn't it be nice if whenever we messed up our life we could simply press *ctrl alt delete* and start over again? *Unknown*

To regret one's own experiences is to arrest one's own development. To deny one's own experiences is to put a lie into the lips of one's life. It is no less than a denial of the soul. *Oscar Wilde*

resentment
Resentment is the poison you drink in the hopes of harming another. *Unknown*

reward
He who wishes to secure the good of others has already secured his own. *Confucius*

right
Human beings are perhaps never more frightening than when they are convinced beyond doubt that they are right. *Laurens Van der Post*

river
You cannot step into a river twice in the same place. *Heraclitus*

rules
Hell, there are no rules here—we're trying to accomplish something. *Thomas A. Edison*

science
Our scientific power has outrun our spiritual power. We have guided missiles and misguided men. *Martin Luther King*

security
Security is mostly superstition. It does not exist in nature. Life is either a daring adventure, or it is nothing. *Helen Keller*

seeing in the dark
I can see, and that is why I can be happy, in what you call the dark, but which to me is golden. I can see a God-made world, not a man-made world. *Helen Keller*

self
This above all. To thine own self be true. And it must follow as the night, the day, thou canst not then be false to any man. *William Shakespeare, Hamlet*

separate
A human being (…) experiences himself, his thoughts and feelings, as something separated from the rest… a kind of optical delusion of his consciousness. This delusion is kind of a prison for us, restricting us to our personal desire and to affection for a few persons nearest us. *Albert Einstein*

sex
Children should never discuss sex in the presence of their elders. *Gregory Nunn*

It has to be admitted that we English have sex on the brain, which is a very unfortunate place to have it. *Malcolm Muggeridge*

Of all sexual aberrations, chastity is the strangest. *Anatole France*

Sexual intercourse is a grossly overrated pastime; the position is undignified, the pleasure momentary and the consequences utterly damnable. *Lord Chesterfield*

"The Holy Spirit leaves the room when a married couple has sex, even if they do it without passion to make new virgins for the kingdom of heaven." *Peter Lombard, theologian 1100-1164*

sexual rivalry
A woman without a man is like a fish without a bicycle. *Gloria Steinem*

No-one should have to dance backward all their lives. *Jill Ruckelshaus*

sexual harassment
Is sexual harassment at work a problem for the self-employed? *Unknown*

simplicity
Simplicity is the ultimate sophistication. *Leonardo da Vinci*

sincerity
A little sincerity is a dangerous thing, and a great deal of it is absolutely fatal. *Oscar Wilde*

speech
For thought is a bird of space, that in a cage of words may indeed unfold its wings but cannot fly. *Kahlil Gibran*

Speech is a faculty given to man to conceal his thoughts. *Talleyrand*

spiritual
We are not human beings having a spiritual experience. We are spiritual beings having a human experience. *Teilhard de Chardin*

statistics
Statistics are like a bikini. What they reveal is suggestive, but what they conceal is vital. *Aaron Levenstein*

strive
All men should strive to learn before they die—what they are running from, and to, and why. *James Thurber*

success
Success is not a matter of spontaneous combustion. You have to set yourself alight. *Abraham Lincoln*

surrealism
How many surrealists does it take to screw in a light bulb? Two: one to hold the giraffe and the other to fill the bathtub with machine tools. *Unknown.*

tact
Tact is the ability to describe others as they see themselves. *Abraham Lincoln*

television
I find television very educating. Every time somebody turns on the set I go into the other room and read a book. *Groucho Marx*

temptation
No man is matriculated to the art of life till he has been well tempted. *George Eliot*

Those who flee temptation generally leave a forwarding address. *Lane Olinghouse*

travel
Travel is fatal to prejudice, bigotry and narrow-mindedness. *Mark Twain*

truth & lies
And if you would know God, be not therefore a solver of riddles. Rather look about you and you shall see Him playing with your children. *Kahlil Gibran*

A thing is not necessarily true because a man dies for it. *Oscar Wilde*

unembarassable
No matter. The dead bird does not leave the nest. *Winston Churchill* (when someone told him his flies were undone.)

universe
The universe begins to look more like a great thought than like a great machine. Mind no longer appears as an accidental intruder in the realm of matter." *James Jeans* 1930

war
War does not determine who is right. It determines who is left. *Unknown*

wealth
I'm living so far beyond my income that we may almost be said to be living apart. *e e cummings*

If you want to get rich from writing, write the sort of thing that's read by persons who move their lips when they're reading to themselves. *Don Marquis*

I've been across the Sahara on a camel, I've been down the Amazon in a canoe, I've been shot in Sarajevo. These are my riches. *Margaret Moth, successful freelance camera operator* (when asked why she wasn't wealthy).

wisdom
You can tell whether a man is clever by his answers. You can tell whether a man is wise by his questions. *Naguib Mahfouz*

Somewhere, something incredible is waiting to be known. *Carl Sagan*

That which seems the height of absurdity in one generation often becomes the height of wisdom in another. *Adlai Stevenson*

wit
Wit is a sword; it is meant to make people feel the point as well as see it. *G.K.Chesterton*

work
Work is the refuge of people who have nothing better to do. *Oscar Wilde*

writer's block
Every morning I get out of bed and I say, "Please God, send me writer's block," and he puts on a stern face and says, "Work you bastard." So I do. *Alan Sillitoe*

BIBLIOGRAPHY

Damasio, Antonio, *Descartes' Error*, Papermac, U.K., 1996.

Winston, Robert, *The Human Mind*, Bantam Press, UK, 2004.

Goleman, Daniel, *Emotional Intelligence*, Bloomsbury, London, 1995.

Gray, Malcolm, *Public Speaking*, Schwartz and Wilkinson, Melbourne, 1991.

Covey, Stephen R., *Seven Habits of Highly Effective People*. The Business Library, Melbourne, 1993.

Humes, James C., *The Language of Leadership*, The Business Library, Melbourne, 1991.

Brown, Ralph McK., *Success at work and at home*, Media Associates, Christchurch, 2004.

Mehrabian, Albert & Ferris, Susan, *Inference of attitudes from nonverbal communication in two channels*. Journal of Consulting Psychology, 1967, Vol. 31, No. 3, 248-252.

Toogood, Granville N., *The Articulate Executive*, McGraw-Hill, 1995.

Mehrabian, Albert & Weiner, Moreton, *Decoding of inconsistent communications*. Journal of Personality and Social Psychology, 1967, Vol. 6, No. 1, 100-114.

Moss, Geoffrey., *Ways with words*, Government Printer, Wellington, 1980

www.media-associates.co.nz